PERUVIAN COOKBOOK

A Simple Guide To Cook Authentic & Traditional Peruvian Recipes at Home Right Now

Miguel Solarzano

Warning-Disclaimer

This Peruvian Cookbook aims to give people ideas about Peruvian recipes. We cannot guarantee that everyone will be successful by following the book.

CONTENTS

Introduction

Peru is a beautiful country located in the western part of South America. It is known for its rich history, diverse culture, stunning natural scenery, and delicious cuisine. Peru is the third-largest country in South America, with a population of over 32 million. Its capital city is Lima, also the country's largest city.

Peru has a fascinating history that spans over 5,000 years. It was once the center of the Inca Empire, the largest empire in pre-Columbian America. The Inca Empire was known for its impressive architecture, including the famous Machu Picchu, a citadel on a mountain ridge beyond the Sacred Valley. The ruins of Machu Picchu attract millions of tourists annually and are considered one of the Seven Wonders of the World.

Peruvian culture is a blend of Spanish and indigenous traditions. The country has 24 official languages, with Spanish being the most widely spoken. The indigenous Quechua language is also widely spoken, especially in the Andean regions. Peruvian music and dance are colorful and lively, with the most famous being the marinera, a traditional dance that originated in the northern coastal regions. Peruvian cuisine is also world-renowned, with dishes such as ceviche, lomo saltado, and pollo a la brasa being famous around the globe.

Peru is a country with an incredibly diverse geography. It is home to the Andes mountain range, the Amazon rainforest, and the Pacific coast. The Andes are the most extended mountain range in the world and run through the center of Peru. The highest peak in Peru is Mount Huascarán, 6,768 meters. The Amazon rainforest covers over 60% of Peru's territory and is one of the most biodiverse places on the planet. The Pacaya-Samiria National Reserve is the largest protected area in Peru and is home to a vast array of wildlife, including monkeys, jaguars, and pink river dolphins. With its natural beauty, Peru has a vibrant economy primarily driven by the mining and tourism industries. Peru is the world's second-largest producer of silver and the third-largest producer of copper. The country is also home to numerous archaeological sites and museums that showcase its rich history and culture. The Larco Museum in Lima is the most famous museum, which houses one of the world's largest collections of pre-Columbian art.

Despite its many achievements, Peru still faces numerous challenges, including poverty, inequality, and corruption. The country's economy has been affected by the COVID-19 pandemic, which has conducted to job losses and decreased economic growth. However, Peru has a resilient population that is committed to improving the country's future. The government has implemented numerous social programs to address poverty and inequality, and many organizations are working to promote sustainable tourism and protect the environment.

Peru is a remarkable country with a rich history, diverse culture, stunning natural scenery, and delicious cuisine. Its people are proud of their heritage and are working hard to build a better future for themselves and their country. Peru is a destination that should be on everyone's bucket list, whether you are interested in exploring ancient ruins, hiking through the mountains, or trying new foods.

PERUVIAN CUISINE

Peru is a country that is renowned for its rich and diverse culinary culture. From the coast to the mountains and the Amazon, the country boasts various ingredients, flavors, and cooking techniques that reflect its diverse history and culture. Peruvian cuisine uniquely blends indigenous, African, European, and Asian influences, making it one of the world's most varied and exciting culinary scenes.

Peruvian cuisine offers something for everyone with various ingredients, including seafood, potatoes, corn, quinoa, and chilies.
The cuisine of Peru has a long history that dates back to pre-Columbian times when the Incas ruled the country. The Inca Empire was a powerful and sophisticated civilization that developed sophisticated farming techniques, including terrace farming, which permitted them to grow crops in the Andean mountains. The Incas also domesticated animals, such as llamas, guinea pigs, and alpacas, used for meat and wool.

After the Spanish domination of Peru in the 16th century, European influences began to shape Peruvian cuisine. The Spanish introduced new ingredients such as garlic, onions, and citrus fruits and cooking techniques such as frying and baking. They also brought enslaved Africans, who brought their culinary traditions to the country. The enslaved Africans introduced new ingredients, such as yams, peanuts, and okra, and cooking techniques, such as frying and stewing.

In the 19th century, Chinese immigrants came to Peru to work in the mines and plantations. The Chinese immigrants brought their culinary traditions, including stir-frying and soy sauce. Chinese immigrants also introduced new ingredients such as ginger, soy sauce, and oyster sauce.

Fusing these different culinary traditions has resulted in a unique, exciting, distinct Peruvian cuisine. Peruvian cuisine is known for its bold flavors and unique combinations of ingredients. One of the most famous foods in Peruvian cuisine is ceviche, a dish made with raw fish marinated in citrus juice and filled with onions and chilies. Other popular dishes include lomo saltado, a stir-fry made with beef, onions, and tomatoes, and causa, a dish made with mashed potatoes, avocado, and seafood.

Peruvian cuisine also features a wide range of indigenous ingredients used in the country for centuries. One of the most essential ingredients is quinoa, a grain high in protein and cultivated in the Andes for thousands of years. Quinoa is used in various dishes, including salads, stews, and soups.

Another essential indigenous ingredient is ají, a spicy chili pepper in many Peruvian dishes. Ají comes in many different varieties, each with its distinct flavor and heat level. The most popular type is the ají amarillo, which is bright yellow and has a fruity, slightly sweet taste.

Potatoes are another essential indigenous ingredient in Peruvian cuisine. Peru is home to over 4,000 varieties of potatoes, many of which are only found here. Potatoes are used in various dishes, including stews, soups, and salads.
Peruvian cuisine is also known for its street food. In cities like Lima, vendors sell snacks and small dishes perfect for a quick bite. Some famous street foods include anticuchos, grilled beef hearts on a stick, picarones, sweet potato, and squash doughnuts served with a syrup made from molasses and figs.

Peruvian cuisine has gained international recognition recently, with many of the country's chefs and restaurants receiving awards and accolades worldwide.

WHY PERUVIAN CUISINE

Peruvian cuisine is a unique fusion of flavors and ingredients that reflects the country's diverse history and geography. With influences from Spanish, African, Asian, and indigenous cultures, Peruvian cuisine reflects multiculturalism and is gaining worldwide recognition for its uncommon and delicious flavors.

Peruvian cuisine has its roots in the Incan empire, where the main staple was maize, potatoes, and other root vegetables. These crops were grown in the highlands and provided the essential ingredients for many Peruvian dishes that are still enjoyed today. With the arrival of Spanish colonizers in the 16th century, new components such as wheat, rice, and various meats were introduced, giving rise to a unique cuisine blending Spanish and indigenous flavors.

One of the most iconic plates of Peruvian cuisine is ceviche, a dish made of raw fish marinated in citrus juice, chilies, and onions. The sharpness of the citrus juice "cooks" the fish, resulting in a delicious and refreshing dish that is perfect for warm weather. Ceviche has been declared part of Peru's national heritage and is considered one of the country's most critical culinary exports.

Another popular dish in Peruvian cuisine is lomo saltado, a stir-fry dish that combines beef, onions, tomatoes, and spices. It is usually filled with rice and French fries, reflecting the influence of Chinese immigrants who came to Peru in the 19th century. Chifa, the name given to Peruvian-Chinese cuisine, has become a staple in the country, giving rise to many unique dishes that combine Chinese cooking techniques with Peruvian ingredients.

Peruvian cuisine also includes various soups, such as chupe de camarones. This creamy shrimp soup is flavored with aji amarillo, a Peruvian chili pepper, and served with potatoes and corn. Another famous soup is the papa a la huancaína, made with boiled potatoes topped with a creamy cheese sauce and garnished with olives and hard-boiled eggs.

Peruvian desserts are also noteworthy, with many recipes passed down from generation to generation. One of the most famous is the suspiro limeño, a dessert made with dulce de leche, meringue, and cinnamon. The name "suspiro" means "sigh" in Spanish, reflecting the dessert's creamy and decadent texture.

In recent years, Peruvian cuisine has gained worldwide recognition, with many of its dishes and ingredients making their way onto menus in some of the world's most famous restaurants. This popularity is partly due to the country's diverse and unique elements, such as quinoa, a superfood that has become popular worldwide, and the aji amarillo, a chili pepper that adds a distinctive flavor and heat to many Peruvian dishes.

Peru's diverse geography has also played a role in shaping the country's cuisine. The Pacific coast provides an abundance of seafood, while the Andean highlands offer a variety of potatoes, grains, and meats. The Amazon rainforest is also a source of unique ingredients, such as fruits and spices, incorporated into Peruvian cuisine.

Peruvian cuisine is a remarkable blend of flavors and ingredients that reflect the country's diverse history and geography. With its indigenous, Spanish, African, and Asian influences, Peruvian cuisine offers a culinary experience. From ceviche to lomo saltado to suspiro limeño, Peruvian cuisine is a must-try for anyone who treasures food and wants to experience the rich cultural heritage of Peru.

PERUVIAN FOOD HISTORY

Peruvian cuisine is among the most diverse and delicious in the world, with a rich history reflecting the country's vibrant and complex cultural heritage. From the Andes peaks to the Amazon rainforest, Peru's varied geography and climate have given rise to various ingredients and culinary traditions shaped by centuries of migration, trade, and colonialism.

The roots of Peruvian cuisine can be traced back to pre-Columbian times when the Incas and other indigenous peoples developed sophisticated farming and culinary techniques that allowed them to thrive in the Andean highlands. Potatoes, quinoa, maize, and other Andean staples were cultivated and consumed in various dishes, often accompanied by alpaca, guinea pig, and other meats.

The arrival of the Spanish in the 16th century brought about significant changes to Peruvian cuisine, as European ingredients such as wheat, rice, and sugar were introduced to the region. Spanish-style stews, soups, and other dishes were also adapted to incorporate local elements, resulting in new hybrid words such as ají de gallina (a spicy chicken stew) and arroz con pollo (chicken and rice).

In the following centuries, Peru became a melting pot of different cultures and cuisines as enslaved Africans, Chinese and Japanese immigrants, and other groups arrived and brought their culinary traditions with them. Enslaved Africans introduced new spices and techniques, such as frying, which led to the creation of dishes such as anticuchos (grilled beef heart skewers) and chicharrón (deep-fried pork). Chinese immigrants brought stir-fry techniques and introduced new ingredients, such as soy sauce and ginger, which led to the creation of dishes such as lomo saltado (e.g.:stir-fried beef with vegetables and rice).

Japanese immigrants arrived in Peru in the late 19th and early 20th centuries and established a thriving community in Lima, the capital city. They introduced sushi, sashimi, and other Japanese dishes, adapted to incorporate local ingredients such as avocado and ají peppers. This fusion of Japanese and Peruvian cuisine became known as Nikkei cuisine, which is now popular worldwide.

Peruvian cuisine received international recognition in the 20th century, thanks in part to the efforts of chefs such as Gastón Acurio and Virgilio Martínez, who have brought Peruvian dishes to the forefront of the global culinary scene. Acurio, in particular, has been instrumental in promoting Peruvian cuisine and ingredients through his restaurants and television shows, which have helped to raise awareness of the country's culinary heritage.

Today, Peruvian cuisine is celebrated for its bold flavors, innovative techniques, and use of diverse ingredients. Ceviche, a food of raw fish marinated in lime juice and ají peppers, has become a symbol of Peruvian cuisine worldwide and is now enjoyed in restaurants and homes across the globe. Other popular dishes include:

- ❖ Causa (a layered potato dish with seafood or chicken).
- ❖ Pachamanca (a traditional Andean dish of meat, vegetables, and herbs cooked in an underground pit).
- ❖ Rocoto relleno (a spicy stuffed pepper dish).

Peruvian cuisine also incorporates a wide range of herbs and spices, such as huacatay (a Peruvian black mint), cumin, oregano, and ají peppers, which lend a unique and complex flavor to dishes.

Beverages such as chicha (a fermented corn drink), pisco (a grape brandy), and Inca Kola (a bright yellow soda) are also an integral part of Peruvian cuisine and culture.

In recent years, Peruvian cuisine has continued to evolve and adapt, incorporating new techniques and ingredients while preserving traditional dishes.

PERUVIAN FOOD LIST

Peruvian cuisine uniquely blends indigenous flavors and cooking techniques with Spanish, African, Chinese, and Japanese influences. It is considered one of the world's most diverse and delicious cuisines, offering various dishes that appeal to all tastes. This article will list some of the most popular Peruvian dishes.

Ceviche
Ceviche is Peru's national dish from fresh raw fish marinated in lime juice, salt, and chili peppers. It is usually served with onions, sweet potato, and corn on the cob. Ceviche is a light and stimulating dish perfect for hot summer days.

Lomo Saltado
Lomo Saltado is a popular Peruvian dish with stir-fried beef strips, onions, tomatoes, and French fries. It is served with rice and is often considered a comfort food in Peru.

Aji de Gallina
Aji de Gallina is a creamy chicken stew with yellow chili peppers, bread crumbs, and milk. It is typically served with boiled potatoes, white rice, and olives.

Anticuchos
Anticuchos are skewers of grilled beef hearts marinated in vinegar, cumin, and garlic. They are often served with boiled potatoes, corn, and spicy salsa.

Papa a la Huancaína
Papa a la Huancaína is a dish of boiled potatoes covered in a creamy cheese sauce made from queso fresco, aji amarillo, and evaporated milk. It is often served as an appetizer.

Rocoto Relleno

Rocoto Relleno is a spicy stuffed pepper dish made with rocoto peppers (Peruvian chili), ground beef, onions, and cheese. It is typically served with potatoes and a salad.

Arroz con Pollo

Arroz con Pollo is a classic Peruvian dish made with rice and chicken. The chicken is usually marinated in garlic and cumin and then cooked with rice, peas, carrots, and other vegetables.

Chupe de Camarones

Chupe de Camarones is a shrimp chowder made with milk, potatoes, corn, cheese, and various spices. It is often served with white rice and avocado.

Causa Rellena

Causa Rellena is a dish of mashed yellow potatoes layered with avocado, tuna or chicken, and mayonnaise. It is often served as an appetizer or a light meal.

Pollo a la Brasa

Pollo a la Brasa is a fully roasted chicken dish marinated in spices, including cumin, garlic, and paprika. It is typically served with French fries(potato fries) and a side of salad.

Chifa

Chifa is Peruvian-Chinese fusion cuisine that originated in Lima's Chinatown. It includes dishes such as fried rice, wontons, and stir-fried noodles.

Cuy

Cuy is a traditional Peruvian dish made with roasted guinea pig. It is often served with potatoes and a spicy sauce.

Picarones

Picarones are Peruvian doughnuts made from sweet potato and

pumpkin served with syrup from chancaca (unrefined cane sugar).

Churros

Churros are a popular dessert in Peru, consisting of fried dough with sugar and cinnamon.

Tres Leches Cake

Tres Leches Cake is a leech cake soaked in three types: evaporated, condensed, and heavy cream. It is often topped with whipped cream and fresh fruit.

PERUVIAN PANTRY LIST

Peruvian cuisine is known for its diverse flavors, unique ingredients, and fusion of indigenous and colonial influences. The country's rich culinary history has created a pantry filled with various essential components essential to Peruvian cooking. This article will analyze a comprehensive list of Peruvian pantry essentials.

Aji Amarillo: Aji Amarillo is a yellow chili pepper that is one of the most essential ingredients in Peruvian cuisine. It is used in sauces, stews, soups, and marinades, adding a spicy and fruity flavor.

Aji Panca: Aji Panca is another chili pepper used in Peruvian cooking. It has a mild, smoky flavor and is often used in stews, soups, and marinades.

Cumin: Cumin is a spice generally used in Peruvian cuisine. It is used in meat dishes, stews, and soups and adds a warm, earthy flavor to dishes.

Huacatay: Huacatay, also known as Peruvian black mint, is a herb used in Peruvian cooking. It is often used in sauces and marinades and has a unique flavor that is a cross between mint and basil.

Paprika: Paprika is a spice often used in Peruvian dishes to add color and flavor. It is used in stews, soups, and marinades and has a sweet and smoky flavor.

Quinoa: Quinoa is a grain that is native to Peru and is often used in Peruvian cuisine. It is used in salads, stews, and soups and is an excellent source of protein and fiber.

Sweet potatoes: Sweet potatoes are a brand in Peruvian cuisine used in various dishes, including stews, soups, and salads. They are sweet and have a creamy texture.

Plantains: Plantains are another staple in Peruvian cuisine used in various dishes. They are often fried and served as a side dish or used to make plantain chips.

Lima beans: Lima beans are a kind of bean that is commonly used in Peruvian cuisine. They are used in stews and soups and have a buttery flavor.

Choclo: Choclo is a corn type used in Peruvian cuisine. It is often boiled, served as a side dish, or used in stews and soups.

Rocoto: Rocoto is a type of chili pepper that is native to Peru. It has a spicy and fruity flavor and is often used in sauces and marinades.

Cilantro: Cilantro is an herb that is usually used in Peruvian cuisine. It is used in sauces, stews, and soups and adds a fresh and citrusy flavor to dishes.

Pisco: Pisco is a type of brandy that is native to Peru. It is often used in cocktails and is a critical ingredient in the national drink of Peru, the Pisco Sour.

Ceviche Mix: Ceviche is a popular dish in Peruvian cuisine made with raw fish marinated in citrus juices. Ceviche mix is a combination of lime juice, salt, and pepper that is used to marinate the fish.

✗ RECIPES ✗

QUINOA PUDDING

Prep Time: 5 mins
Cook Time: 30 mins
Total Time: 35 mins

Ingredients

- 1 ½ cups water
- ¾ cup quinoa
- Two tablespoons white sugar
- salt to taste
- ½ tablespoon butter
- 2 cups whole milk
- Two ripe bananas
- ½ teaspoon vanilla extract

Directions

Quinoa should be rinsed and drained. In a saucepan over high heat, bring water and quinoa to a boil while stirring periodically. For 15 minutes, simmer with the heat down and the lid on. Get rid of the heat.

In a food processor, combine the milk, bananas, sugar, and salt and pulse until completely smooth. Add the milk mixture to the quinoa in the pan.

Set the pan over a medium heat source. Cook and whisk the mixture for 5 to 10 minutes or until it turns thick and creamy. Get rid of the heat. Serve warm after adding the butter and vanilla.

YUCA FRIES

Prep Time: 15 mins
Cook Time: 30 mins
Total Time: 45 mins
Servings: 4 servings

Equipment

- Pot
- Baking Sheet
- Skillet

Ingredients

- 1 ½ pounds fresh yuca
- One teaspoon salt
- Spicy Aioli
- 2 cups vegetable oil
- 5 cups water

Directions

Cut the yuca in half lengthwise after peeling it. From the center, cut off and discard the stem. Fill a medium-sized saucepan with the yuca. Add salt and water. After bringing to a boil, cook for 15 to 20 minutes over medium-high heat. Yuca should be taken out of the water. With paper towels, pat the yuca to dry. Cut them into long, 1-2 inch pieces that are 1/2 inch thick.

On medium-high heat, heat the oil in a medium skillet. The yuca must be fried on each side for two to three minutes or until crispy and golden. Transfer all to a plate lined with paper towels/tissue to drain any extra grease. Serve hot with aioli sauce that is fresh for dipping.

Notes

I like to boil the yuca before frying it to ensure a soft core. The yuca may be fried without scorching it, though. To ensure they are well cooked, reduce the heat to medium when frying.

To prevent oil splatters, dry the yuca with paper towels before frying. Instead of frying the yuca, bake it by spreading the yuca fingers on a baking sheet and roasting them at 425 degrees for 20 to 24 mins or until golden brown, flipping the pan midway through.

WONTON SOUP

Prep Time: 30 mins
Cook Time: 10 mins
Additional Time: 25 mins
Total Time: 1 hrs 5 mins

Ingredients

Wontons:
- ½ pound boneless pork loin, coarsely chopped
- 2 ounces peeled shrimp, finely chopped
- One teaspoon of brown sugar
- One teaspoon of finely chopped green onions
- One tablespoon of Chinese rice wine
- One tablespoon of light soy sauce
- One teaspoon of chopped fresh ginger root
- 24 (3.5-inch square) wonton wrappers

Soup:
- 3 cups chicken stock
- Two tablespoons finely chopped green onions

Directions

Making the wontons:
Mix the pork, shrimp, rice wine, soy sauce, green onions, brown sugar, and ginger in a large bowl. For 25 to 30 minutes, let it stand.

A teaspoon of filling must be placed in the middle of each wonton wrapper. Fold the filling to form a triangle; press the sides tightly to seal. Moisten all four wrapper edges with water. Above the filling, bring the left and right corners together. Overlap the tips of these corners, wet them with water, and then press them together to form a seal. Continue until every wrapper has been filled and sealed.

Produce the soup: Bring chicken stock to a rolling boil in a pot. Add the wontons carefully, then cook for 5 minutes.Add green onions as a garnish after ladling into dishes.

Notes

If properly covered, uncooked wontons can be stored in the freezer for up to two months. If boiling them, drop frozen wontons into boiling soup and let them cool for 7 minutes. If you're frying them, thaw them beforehand.

Heat 2/3 cups of oil in a wok to fry wontons. Wontons must be fried in batches until golden, about 2 to 3 minutes on each side. Drain on a platter covered with towels. Serve with any dipping sauce, including duck sauce (plum sauce).

CHICKEN LIVER CURRY

Prep Time: 15 minutes
Cook Time: 15 minutes
Total Time: 30 minutes
Servings: 3

Equipment
- Saucepan
- Mixing pot

Ingredients
- 600 grams of chicken livers
- Two pieces of chopped onions
- 1 tbsp chicken masala or garam masala
- 1/2 tbsp coriander powder
- 1/2 tbsp cumin seeds

- 2 tbsp finely chopped coriander powder
- Two pieces medium size chopped tomatoes
- 1 tbsp ginger-garlic paste
- 1 tbsp chopped green chili
- 1 tbsp red chili powder
- 1/2 tbsp black pepper powder
- salt as per taste
- cooking oil

Directions

Heat 2-3 tsp cooking oil in a saucepan with medium flame. After enough heat, oil:

1. Take ½ tsp cumin seeds and add these to the oil.
2. Sauté it until it turns light red.
3. Add chopped green chili and onion to the saucepan.
4. Add salt and Sauté them for 3-4 minutes.

While the onion turns light brown, add all the spices (except sliced green chili and coriander leaves) and sauté for 5 minutes.

Add chopped tomatoes and stir a little, then close the saucepan lid. Cook it for five minutes, then open the cover. Add chicken liver and stir for 5-6 minutes or up to change the color, then add ½ cup water and close the lid again.

Cook it for 10-12 minutes, then open the lid and add sliced green chili and coriander leaves. Stir a little to mix them, then turn off the flame. The dish is now ready to serve.

APPLE EMPANADAS

Prep Time: 15 mins
Cook Time: 30 mins
Total Time: 45 mins
Servings: 6 servings

Ingredients

For the Filling
- Four large Rave apples, peeled and diced
- One tablespoon of lime juice
- One teaspoon vanilla
- One tablespoon cornstarch
- ½ cup brown sugar
- ½ teaspoon ground cinnamon
- ¼ teaspoon ground nutmeg
- Pinch of salt

For the Empanadas
- One pack (2 crusts) of refrigerated pie dough
- One egg, for egg wash
- Turbinado sugar

Directions

Preheat oven to 450 degrees F. Add Rave apples, lime juice, sugar, cinnamon, nutmeg, and vanilla into a small pot. Over medium-high heat, cook the apples, stirring occasionally, until they are tender, about 15-20 minutes. They should have soaked up a lot of the liquid. Add cornstarch and stir. Transfer into a bowl and set it aside to cool.

Place pastry dough on a flat, lightly floured surface, stack pie crusts, and roll out to a ¼-inch thick. Cut out four circles using a small bowl or a 6" round cutter—re-roll scraps to cut out two additional rounds. Include about one tablespoon of the apple filling in the center of each dough round. Brush the egg around the edges of each round.

Fold one side of the dough over and press the edges together using a fork until fully sealed. You can also press the edges together by pinching the sides using your index finger. Make sure that they are fully closed. Line 2-3 baking sheets with paper (parchment) and place the empanadas on top.

Cut a few small slits on the top of each empanada with a short knife to let the steam out while baking. Brush (plastic handle brush) the tops with the egg, and sprinkle with turbinado sugar. Bake until the pastry is golden, for about 10-12 minutes.

Notes

Wait to cook the apples on too high a heat, or they will stick to the bottom of the pan. Let the apple mixture cool before placing it into the empanada dough.Make a slit on the top of each empanada so that the steam can escape. If you don't do this, they can burst during baking. Cook the empanadas on parchment for easy removal.

QUINOA VEGETABLE STEW

Prep Time: 15 mins
Cook Time: 40 mins
Total Time: 55 mins
Servings: 6

Ingredients
- 2 Tbsp olive oil
- One onion, chopped
- 6 cups low-sodium vegetable broth
- One lb. red potatoes, unpeeled, cut into 1/2-inch pieces
- 1 cup white quinoa, well-rinsed and drained
- 1 cup fresh or frozen corn
- Two tomatoes, cored and chopped coarsely
- 1 cup frozen peas
- One red bell pepper stemmed, seeded, and cut into 1/2-inch pieces
- Five garlic minced

- 4 oz feta cheese crumbled
- One avocado, halved, pitted
- 1/2 cup chopped fresh cilantro
- 1 Tbsp paprika
- 2 tsp ground coriander
- 1 1/2 tsp ground cumin
- Salt and pepper

Directions

In an oven, heat the oil over medium heat. Include the onion and bell pepper and cook for about 5 minutes or until soft.

Add the garlic, paprika, cumin, and coriander, and stir for approximately 30 seconds until aromatic. Add the potatoes and broth after mixing, then heat to a boil. Lessen the heat to medium, cover the pot, and simmer gently for 10 minutes.

For 8 minutes, stir in the quinoa and simmer. Since I used frozen corn, I added the corn after the peas and simmered for 5 to 7 minutes, or until the potatoes and quinoa were soft.

Add the tomatoes and peas and stir. Cook for 2 minutes or until heated through. Include salt and pepper to taste, and turn the heat off. Before serving, top each portion with queso fresco, avocado, and cilantro.

Notes

The toppings are essential to the flavor of this soup; do not leave them out. The stew may be kept in the fridge for up to 2 days; add liquid to thin the sauce before warming.

APPLE CRISP

Prep Time: 30 mins
Cook Time: 45 mins
Total Time: 1 hrs 15 mins

Ingredients

- 10 cups apples, peeled, cored and sliced
- 1 cup white sugar
- 1 cup all-purpose flour
- 1 cup packed brown sugar
- ¼ teaspoon baking powder
- One tablespoon of all-purpose flour
- One teaspoon of ground cinnamon
- ½ cup water
- 1 cup quick-cooking oats
- ¼ teaspoon baking soda
- ½ cup melted butter

Directions

Gather all ingredients. The oven must be preheated at 175 degrees C. A 9x13-inch baking dish should be filled with apple slices. Sprinkle apples with white sugar, cinnamon, and one tablespoon of flour. Over the fruits, equally, distribute water.

Combine the oats,1 cup flour, brown sugar, baking powder, and soda in a large region. After adding the melted butter spread the crumbled butter mixture evenly over the apple mixture.

Bake for about 45 minutes until the apples are bubbling around the edges and the top is golden brown.

CHICKEN SOUP

Prep time: 15 mins
Cook time: 35 mins
Servings: 4

Ingredients

- 1 tbsp olive oil
- Two chopped onions
- 300g leftover roast chicken, shredded and skin removed
- 200g frozen peas
- 3 tbsp Greek yogurt
- One garlic clove, crushed
- Three medium-chopped carrots
- 1 tbsp chopped thyme leaves
- 1.4l chicken stock
- squeeze lemon juice
- cheese scone to serve

Direction

In a large pan with a thick base, heat the olive oil. For 15 minutes, gently sauté the onions, carrots, and thyme leaves. Add the 1.4 liters of chicken stock and stir. Bring to a boil.Add the remaining roast chicken, divide the mixture in half, and blend with a stick blender until smooth. Put the remainder of the soup, the peas, and the spice back into the pan and stir. Simmer for 5 minutes or until well heated.

Combine the Greek yogurt, lemon juice, and garlic. Pour the soup into bowls, stir in the yogurt with the garlic, and then serve. If using a slow cooker, gently sauté the onions, carrots, and thyme leaves for 15 minutes before adding 1 liter of liquid to the pot.Add the chicken carcass now if you're using one. The vegetables should be soft after 2-3 hours on High while covered.

If you used a carcass, remove it immediately and shred any chicken still on the bones. Add the frozen peas and leftover roast chicken to the broth or stir them back in.Thirty more minutes of cooking.
Serving as before, take half of the mixture out and purée with a stick blender.

PUMPKIN SOUP

Prep Time: 20 mins
cook Time: 25 mins
Servings: 6

Ingredients

- 2 tbsp olive oil
- Two onions, chopped
- 150ml double cream
- 1kg pumpkin or squash, peeled, deseeded, and chopped into chunks
- 700ml vegetable stock or chicken stock
- For the croutons
- 2 tbsp olive oil
- handful pumpkin seeds
- Four slices wholemeal seeded bread, crusts removed

Direction

In a sizeable saucepan, heat 2 tbsp of olive oil. Then, gently sauté two onions that have been finely diced for 5 minutes until tender but not colored.

One kilogram of cut-up pumpkin or squash should be added to the pan. Cook for 8-10 mins while stirring regularly or until the squash has softened and turned golden.Salt and pepper 700ml of chicken or vegetable stock before adding it to the pan. When the squash is exceptionally tender, simmer for 10 minutes after bringing it to a boil.

150 ml of double cream should be added to the pan, brought back to a boil, and blended with a hand blender. Pass the soup with a fine sieve to create it even more silky. Now, you may freeze the soup for up to two months. Shave four slices of whole-wheat seeded bread into tiny squares to create the croutons.

The bread should be fried in 2 tablespoons of hot olive oil until crisp. After a few more minutes of cooking, you will toast the pumpkin seeds after adding a large handful to the pan. You may prepare these a day in advance and keep them in an airtight jar.

If necessary, reheat the soup, check the seasoning, and then serve it garnished with croutons, seeds, and more olive oil, if desired.

BEAN ESCABECHE

Prep Time: 12hrs
Cook Time: 1 hr 30 mins
Total Time: 13 hrs 30 mins
Servings: 4

Ingredients
- 1 pound canary beans
- 1 pound small red onions
- Six garlic cloves divided
- Two fresh ají amarillo
- One teaspoon of ground cumin
- Salt and pepper
- 1 cup vegetable stock
- One tablespoon ají panca paste
- Three bay leaves
- ½ cup red wine vinegar
- 4 Iceberg lettuce leaves
- Four black olives
- Two hard-boiled eggs, cut in half
- Salt
- ¼ cup olive oil

Directions

Cover the beans with water in a bowl, and let them soak all night. The following day, rinse the beans and add them to a container with enough water to cover them. Carry to a boil, lower the heat to medium, and simmer the beans for an hour, partially covered with a lid, or until tender. To taste, add salt. Heat whole olive oil in a frying pan over medium heat when the beans are finished cooking. Add the aj panca and aj amarillo, bay leaves, vinegar, cumin, salt, and pepper, and the two onions cut into thick slices from root to top. Cook for five minutes before adding the vegetable stock and cook for five.

Put the beans in a serving dish after straining them. Serve on a lettuce leaf with escabeche sauce on top, black olives, and, if preferred, half-hard-boiled eggs as garnishes.

ROAST PERUVIAN TURKEY

Prep Time: 30 mins
Cook Time: 3 hrs 25 mins
Additional Time: 1 hrs 20 mins
Total Time: 5 hrs 15 mins

Ingredients

* 12-pound whole turkey, neck, and giblets removed

Spice rub:

* ½ cup ground cumin
* ½ cup soy sauce
* One tablespoon of smoked paprika
* One tablespoon of dried oregano
* Two teaspoons of kosher salt
* One tablespoon of vegetable oil
* ½ cup white vinegar
* ⅓ cup vegetable oil
* 12 cloves garlic, peeled
* Three tablespoons paprika

- Two tablespoons freshly ground black pepper
- Two teaspoons water

Sauce:
- 8-ounce container of creme fraiche
- 1 cup chicken broth
- Two jalapeno peppers stemmed
- ½ cup chopped fresh cilantro
- salt and freshly ground black pepper
- One pinch of cayenne pepper
- One lime, juiced

Directions

Use paper towels/tissue to pat the turkey dry. With a spatula placed beneath the skin, loosen the skin covering either side of the breastbone.

Blend cumin, oregano, smoked paprika, black pepper, soy sauce, vinegar, vegetable oil, garlic, and paprika.For approximately a minute, blend the spice rub to a thick paste. Pour the remaining rub over the turkey and use a spatula to apply about two tablespoons of the mixture under the loosening skin on each breast. Set aside 1/2 cup of the rub in a basin for a later stage.

The turkey must be covered in the mixture all over. Let the turkey rest at room temperature for an hour. The oven must be preheated to 325 F (165 C).

Set aside a piece of aluminum foil rolled into a spherical shape approximately the size of a turkey breast. Put the turkey on a rack that is inside a big roasting pan. Use kitchen twine to bind the legs together at the bottom.Spread 1/4 cup of the wet rub saved into the turkey cavity; reserve the remaining 1/4 cup for another use. Kosher salt should be applied liberally to the turkey's top and sides.

Put a foil tent over the turkey breast and roast for 1 1/2 hrs in the oven. Re-enter the stove, and cook for a further hour and fifteen minutes. Mix the remaining 1/4 cup of spice rub, one tablespoon of vegetable oil, and water in a separate dish. Brush the mixture over the turkey's top, legs, and sides. Roast for 30 minutes or up to an instant-read meat thermometer put into the thickest part of a thigh that is not touching bone reads 75 to 80 degrees C.

Reserving drippings in a roasting pan, move the turkey to a serving tray, and allow it to rest for at least 20 minutes. Blend the following ingredients in a blender: crème fraiche, chicken broth, lime juice, jalapeño peppers, and cilantro.

Place the roasting pan over a burner set to medium-high heat, remove the extra fat from the pan, add the creme fraiche mixture, and roast the turkey as usual.

Add the browned pan drippings to the sauce mixture, boil, and simmer for 10 minutes or until the gravy has thickened and been reduced by half. Season gravy with black pepper, salt, and cayenne pepper to taste. Whisk often to avoid lumps. Carve the turkey and serve it with pan gravy.

Notes

Roasting time is about 15 minutes per pound or about 3 hours for a 12-pound turkey. Mine was about 13 pounds.

OCOPA SAUCE

Prep Time: 15mins
Cook Time: 25mins
Total Time: 40mins
Servings: 4

Ingredients
- 1/4 cup vegetable oil
- Four red onions, small, sliced
- 8 ounces fresh white cheese
- evaporated milk
- Four garlic cloves, crushed

- Two sprigs huacatay
- Five bell peppers
- 3 gm crackers
- 4 ounces roasted peanuts
- Salt & pepper

Directions

Heat the oil and saute onion, garlic, huacatay, and ají amarillo until well browned. Remove from heat and allow to cool.

In a food processor, coarsely mix the cooled vegetables with the cookies, peanuts, and cheese. Slowly add evaporated milk, if needed, to reach a thick yet durable consistency.

Add salt and pepper to taste. Serve over cold sliced boiled potatoes, garnished with boiled egg slices.

PANETTONE FRENCH TOAST

Prep Time: 8 mins
Cook Time: 20 mins
Total Time: 28 mins
servings: 6

Ingredients
Syrup:
- 1 cup water
- 1/2 teaspoon ground cinnamon
- One packed cup of brown sugar

French Toast:
- 1-pound panettone, paper removed
- Six large eggs
- Two tablespoons unsalted butter divided
- 1/2 cup mascarpone cheese
- Two tablespoons whipping cream
- 3/4 cup whole milk
- 1/4 cup sugar

Directions

For the syrup, boil the water and sugar in a medium saucepan on high heat while stirring until the sugar dissolves.
Boil for 10 minutes or until the syrup is reduced to 1 cup. Whisk in the cream and cinnamon after taking the pan off the heat.

Until you are ready to serve, keep the syrup heated over low heat. (The syrup can be prepared a day in advance. Refrigerate after cooling and covering. Before serving, reheat.

For the French toast:

Set the oven to 200 degrees Fahrenheit. A big nonstick saute pan, or nonstick griddle should be preheated. Remove the panettone's top using a serrated knife.

The panettone's bottom must be cut in half crosswise. Make four equal pieces from both sides. Whisk the eggs, cream, milk, and sugar in a large bowl until well combined. On the griddle, melt one tablespoon of butter. Slices of panettone must be dipped into the custard in phases and turned to let all sides absorb the custard. Cook the soaked panettone slices for 4 minutes on each side or until they are firm to the touch and golden brown.

French toast must be moved to a baking sheet and heated in the oven. Repeat is necessary with the last tablespoon of butter and the panettone pieces.

Move the French toast to serving plates. After drizzling it with the cinnamon syrup, place a dollop of mascarpone on top of the French toast. Serve with fresh berries and sprinkle with powdered sugar.

Notes

The top of the panettone can be reserved and used for toast.

PERUVIAN CAUSA

Prep Time: 20 mins
Cook Time: 20 mins
Additional Time: 50 mins
Total Time: 1 hrs 30 mins

Ingredients

- Eight russet potatoes peeled
- ½ cup vegetable oil
- One small red onion
- ½ cup mayonnaise
- Two avocados, cut into thin strips
- Three hard-boiled eggs
- Two tablespoons minced aji amarillo
- salt and ground black pepper
- 5-ounce tuna

Directions

Put the potatoes in a big saucepan, add salted water, and boil. Simmer for about 20 mins until tender, then reduce heat to medium-low. Drain. Use a ricer or hand mixer to mash potatoes thoroughly. Add aji amarillo, salt, and pepper after adding the oil until the potatoes are combined. Let the potato mixture chill for about 20 minutes in the refrigerator.

Combine the tuna, onion, and 1/4 cup mayonnaise in a bowl. Plastic wrap should be used to line a casserole dish.Spread 1/2 of the potato blend on the bottom of the dish. Spread two tablespoons of mayonnaise over the potatoes, spread the tuna mixture over the mayonnaise, and place the avocado slices in a single layer on top of the tuna mixture.

Spread the remaining 1/2 of the potato mixture over the avocados and top with the two tablespoons of mayonnaise. Place sliced eggs over the top. Wrap the casserole dish with polythene wrap and refrigerate until firm, about 30 minutes.

Invert the casserole dish onto a serving plate or baking sheet to remove the potato casserole from the dish. Remove the plastic wrap and cut the casserole into squares.

POTATO CHEESE SOUP

Prep Time: 10 mins
Cook Time: 15mins
Total time: 25mins
Servings: 4

Ingredients

- Four potatoes peeled
- One small carrot, chopped
- One tablespoon of dried parsley
- One teaspoon of ground black pepper
- 1 cup shredded Swiss cheese
- ½ stalk celery, chopped
- One small onion, minced
- 1 ½ cups vegetable broth
- One teaspoon salt
- 2 ½ cups milk
- Three tablespoons melted butter
- Three tablespoons flour

Directions

Potatoes, carrots, celery, onion, vegetable broth, and salt must boil in a big pot. Reduce heat, cover, and cook potatoes until they are just tender. Don't rinse; mash the mixture just a little. Milk has been added; stir. Add butter, flour, parsley, and pepper to the potato mixture.

When bubbling and thickened, cook and stir over medium heat. Add the cheese and stir with the heat off until it almost melts. Let soup sit for five minutes.

ARROZ CHAUFA

Prep Time: 5 mins
Cook Time: 10 mins
Total Time: 15 mins

Ingredients

- 2 Tbs sesame oil
- One bunch of green onion, chopped
- 4 cups pre-cooked
- 2-3 Tablespoons soy sauce
- One bell pepper
- Two hot dogs
- Two eggs
- Two garlic cloves
- One tablespoon of ginger root
- 1 cup cooked and shredded chicken

Directions

A big skillet or wok must be heated to medium. Sesame oil must be added to the bottom. Add bell pepper, onion, and hot dogs. Include ginger and garlic. Pour the whole beaten eggs onto the other side after sliding to the side. Eggs must be beaten using a spatula. Combine the cooked eggs with the vegetable mixture. For the vegetable and egg mixture, include the rice and chicken. On top, add the soy sauce. The rice and vegetable combination must be stir-fried and cooked thoroughly. To taste, add more salt to the dish.

CARAMEL POPCORN

Prep Time: 15 mins
Cook Time: 1 hrs
Total Time: 1 hrs 15 mins

Ingredients

- 5 quarts of popped popcorn
- 1 cup butter
- One teaspoon of vanilla extract
- ½ teaspoon baking soda
- 2 cups brown sugar
- ½ cup corn syrup
- One teaspoon salt

Directions

Set the oven's temperature to 250 °F (120 °C)—a large bowl filled with popcorn. In a saucepan, place on medium heat, melt the butter. Add salt, corn syrup, and brown sugar after mixing. Stirring continuously, bring to a boil. Boil for four minutes without stirring. Add baking soda and vanilla after removing the pan from the heat. While stirring, pour a thin stream of caramel over the popcorn. Stir to ensure even coating. In two big, shallow baking containers, divide the popcorn. Bake for 1 hr in the preheated oven, stirring every fifteen minutes.

After removing from the oven, let the pieces cool entirely before slicing.

SEAFOOD SOUP RECIPE

Prep Time: 15 mins
Cook Time: 1 hr 40 mins
Total Time: 1 hr 55 mins
Servings: 8

Ingredients

- 2 pounds of assorted fish
- 2 tbsp olive oil to saute vegetables
- 1 tbsp old bay
- 1 tsp sea salt
- ½ tsp black pepper
- 1 tbsp fresh thyme fine chop
- 1 cup celery diced
- 1 cup diced onions
- 1 cup diced carrots
- 2 cups diced potatoes
- 1 cup zucchini diced
- 1 cup corn kernels
- 2 cups plum tomatoes or crushed tomatoes
- 2 quarts chicken stock
- 1 tbsp Italian parsley - chopped garnish

Directions

Add olive oil, celery, onions, and carrots in a large pot over medium-high heat.

Saute for 3-4 minutes, then add the remaining vegetables except for the tomatoes. Continue to cook the veggies over medium heat for 5 - 10 minutes.Reduce the heat to low and let the veggies cook for 10-15 more. After the vegetables have cooked, add the stock, tomatoes, and seasonings to the pot. Carry to a boil, reduce the heat to low, and let the soup simmer for 25 mins.Add the seafood to the pot and continue to simmer for 30 minutes to an hour. Re-season to taste with sea salt and black pepper.

Garnish soup with chopped parsley and serve with your favorite crusty bread.

SALMON CEVICHE

Total: 1 hr 30 mins
Servings: 6

Ingredients

- 1 ½ pounds boned, skinned wild salmon cut into bite-size chunks
- ¾ cup lime juice
- ½ teaspoon dried oregano
- Three. crisp tostada shells
- Two medium tomatoes
- ½ red chopped onion,
- ½ cup coarsely chopped cilantro
- Two tablespoons extra-virgin olive oil
- One pickled jalapeño
- ½ to 1 serrano chile
- One teaspoon of kosher salt

Directions

In a glass container, combine the salmon and lime juice. Let it rest for about 30 minutes, stirring regularly, until the salmon is opaque and slightly stiff. Meanwhile, combine all the remaining components in a separate bowl except the tostada shells. Drain the fish, keeping three tablespoons of the lime juice. Combine the saved tomato mixture with the fish. With tostada shells on the side. In well-stocked Latino stores, you may find little tostada shells.

The 2012 "Bella Flor" Dry Rosé of Syrah from Ceja. This pink, exquisitely crisp, balances the acidic lemon flavors of the ceviche, and its lively red fruit cools the chiles and accentuates the wild salmon. (error recipe) *update next edition*

SPICY CHICKEN SOUP

Prep Time: 10 mins
Cook Time: 50 mins
Total Time: 1 hr
Servings: 6

Ingredients

- 4 cups water
- 1 pound boneless skinless chicken breasts
- 1 Tablespoon olive oil
- 1/2 chopped onion
- Two cloves garlic
- Three teaspoons of chicken bouillon paste
- 8 ounces salsa
- 14.5-ounce can of diced tomatoes
- 4 ounces tomato sauce
- 1/2 Tablespoon granulated sugar
- 2 Tablespoons chili powder
- One teaspoon cumin
- 1/2 teaspoon salt
- One teaspoon of freshly ground black pepper
- One teaspoon of garlic powder
- 1 Tablespoon dried parsley flakes
- Three teaspoons of onion powder
- 15-ounce can of corn (frozen)
- 16-ounce can of chili beans
- 3/4 cup sour cream
- Cilantro, shredded cheese, and avocado for soup garnish

Directions

Combine water, chicken, salt, pepper, garlic powder, parsley, onion powder, and bouillon in a large saucepan over medium heat.
Bring to a boil, lessen the heat, and simmer the chicken for 20 to 30 minutes or until thoroughly cooked.

Shred the chicken, then transfer it to a platter. Set aside 3 1/2 cups of the chicken broth water.

Olive oil is used to sauté onion and garlic in a big saucepan over medium heat until brown.

Add 3 1/2 cups of the conserved water, salsa, tomato sauce, sugar, cumin, chili powder, diced tomatoes, and shredded chicken. For 30 minutes, simmer. Add sour cream and stir. After tasting, add more salt or other spices as needed. Add cilantro, cheese, avocado, crumbled tortilla chips, or whatever you prefer as a garnish!

Notes

Onion and garlic must be sautéed in different batches of oil for the slow cooker. Add all the ingredients excluding the sour cream, to a crock pot, and cook for 5 hrs on low or until the chicken is done. Add sour cream after shredding the chicken.

Use these instructions to add oil to an instant pot set to sauté. Sauté garlic and onion. Sour cream, chili beans, and corn must not be added to the instant pot. After adding all the ingredients, cook on High Pressure for 8 mins with a 10-minute natural release. Combine shredded chicken with beans, corn, and sour cream.

SHRIMP STIR FRY

Prep Time: 15 mins
Cook Time: 20 mins
Total Time: 35 mins
Servings: 4

Ingredients

- 2 tbsp. extra-virgin olive oil
- One lb. shrimp (peeled and deveined)
- 1/2 c. low-sodium soy sauce
- 1 tbsp. cornstarch
- Juice of 1 lime
- 2 tbsp. packed brown sugar
- Pinch red pepper flakes
- Kosher salt
- Freshly ground black pepper
- 1 tbsp. sesame oil
- One small head of broccoli
- Eight oz. sugar snap peas
- One red bell pepper, sliced
- Three cloves garlic, minced
- 1 tbsp. minced ginger

Directions

Heat the olive oil in a sizeable skillet on medium heat. Include the shrimp and salt and pepper to taste. Remove from skillet after 5 minutes of cooking till pink.

Sesame oil is heated in the skillet again. Cook the broccoli, peas, and bell pepper for 7 minutes or until soft. Cook the garlic and ginger for a further minute or until fragrant. Mix the soy sauce, lime juice, cornstarch, brown sugar, and an addition of red pepper flakes. Add to skillet, then coat with a toss. Cook for 2 minutes after adding the shrimp.

MILANESA DE POLLO

Prep Time: 15 mins
Cook Time: 8 mins
Total Time: 23 mins
Servings: 4

Ingredients

- Two eggs
- Salt
- 1 cup bread crumbs
- Two skinless, boneless chicken breast halves
- 1/2 cup oil for frying
- 1/2 teaspoon smoked paprika optional
- 1/4 teaspoon ground chile de arbol
- pepper
- ¾ cup all-purpose flour
- Spices to season bread crumbs:
- 1/2 teaspoon dried oregano
- 1/2 teaspoon ground cumin
- 1/2 teaspoon garlic powder
- 1/2 teaspoon onion powder

Directions

Cut the chicken breast in half, then pound it with a meat tenderizer to make it uniformly thick. Save for later use by placing aside. Add flour to one dish, eggs to another, and bread crumbs to the third dish to create a breading station. The eggs should be seasoned with salt and pepper.

Whirl the eggs. Mix the ingredients with your selected spices with a fork to the bread crumbs. Chicken must be dredged with flour. Clear away any extra flour. After flouring it, add the chicken to the egg mixture. Make sure the egg mixture is all over the chicken. The chicken should next be coated with bread crumbs.

Make sure the bread crumbs cover every inch of the chicken once again. Continue until all of the chicken pieces are covered, then set aside. An oil skillet is heating up. The chicken should be fried in batches for 3 to 4 minutes each side. Using a paper towel, transfer each cooked chicken to a platter. Fry the chicken pieces in batches to they are completely done. Serve with your preferred salsa, french fries, and salad.

Notes

Using a deep fryer, the chicken will cook in about 4 minutes.

Oven use advice:
The oven must be preheated at 190 C. For about 15 minutes, bake the chicken, flipping it over halfway through.

CACHANGS

Dough rest Time: 4 hours
Prep Time:15 mins
Cook Time: 15 mins
Servings: 15

Ingredients

- 500 gm ready-made wheat flour
- Two eggs
- 2 tbsp. butter
- Vegetable oil for frying
- 1 cup of warm water
- 1 tbsp. white or blonde sugar
- 1 tsp salt

Directions

We take a large bowl and sift the flour inside; then we pour the sugar and anise; little by little, it is mixed with a spoon or with our hands to integrate the ingredients thoroughly. Add a pinch of salt with each component immersed in the other and continue mixing.

When all the dry ingredients are integrated, it will be time to add the eggs, and then we will begin to incorporate them to create a somewhat sticky and chewy dough. When this texture is obtained, it will be time to add water. You should add it gently. Then try to form a ball from the dough and do it with your hands.
If the dough is still chewy, you can add flour little by little while wrapping it as if it were forming a snowball. Continue to manipulate the dough by giving it a round shape. The end of this is as it comes into contact with the dough, it leaves the sticky texture and becomes solid, like a plasteline.

Once the dough has a texture like a plasteline, it no longer sticks to your hands; it will be time to let it rest for 4 hours in the same container of origin. Cover such a container with plastic wrap and a rag that cuts off the lighting.
The time in mention is with the intention that the dough is inflated. After time, it will be time to stretch the dough on a table or flat place.

Use flour for the flat base and roll to stretch it. Tear off a piece of the dough into a ball shape and better the circumference when it is isolated. Do this until the large dough ends up divided into several medium balls. Then on a dry and clean base, stretch each ball (one at a time) with the rolling pin until it is the size of an egg omelet.

Now it's time to put oil in a deep pan or wide pot and wait to warm up. When it is hot (5 minutes), it will be time to pour the dough into tortillas. They will take on a larger size independently, and you will have to turn it over every time because cooking is fast, and they can burn. Repeat this until you finish all the masses.

Remember to read a clean container covered on the base with a paper towel to absorb excess fat into the paper.

And that's it! It will be time to enjoy this culinary delight, and you can accompany it with honey, jam, white delicacy, or whatever cream you want. Our additional recommendation is that you attend it with hot coffee or tea.

CHORIPAN WITH TROPICAL SALSA

Prep Time: 20 mins
Cook Time: 10 mins
Total Time: 30 mins
Servings: 1

Ingredients

Salsa:

- ½ cup red beans, cooked
- Two tablespoons onion, diced
- Cilantro leaves
- One tomato
- ½ avocado
- ½ ripe plantain, peeled, fried and diced
- Salt and pepper
- Juice of 1 lemon

Sandwich:

- Two sausages
- 1 Flatout Foldit
- Mayonnaise
- Lettuce leaves
- Mustard
- Chili pepper sauce

Directions

Salsa:
Combine the beans, onion, tomato, avocado, fried plantain, salt, pepper, lime juice, and cilantro leaves.Reserve.

Sandwich:
Cook the sausages in a skillet or grill until cooked. Put the Flatout Foldit on a plate, cover it with a lettuce leaf, and put the links on top. Drizzle with mustard or chili pepper sauce, top with the tropical salsa, fold the Flatbread, and serve immediately.

SPANISH ARROZ CON LECHE RECIPE

Prep Time: 5 mins
Cook Time: 30 mins
Total Time: 35 mins
Servings: 4

Ingredients

- 1 cup of short-grain rice
- 1-2 wide slices of lemon rind
- 1-liter whole milk
- Sugar to taste
- One stick of cinnamon
- One teaspoon of ground cinnamon
- One pinch of salt

Directions

Rinse the rice under cold water and then put it in a saucepan over medium heat, barely covered with water. Add the cinnamon stick and lemon rind. Stir continually until all of the water is absorbed.
Add milk about ½ cup, stirring each time until all is absorbed. Continue adding up to the whole liter of milk, stirring continuously.

When it seems creamy enough, taste it to make sure the texture of the rice is correct. Some prefer it al dente, and others like it very cooked.

Please turn off the heat and add salt and a dash of cinnamon when you like. Then, add the sugar a few tablespoons until it is sweet enough for you. Enjoy warm or let cool.

Notes

Always use whole milk for the best flavor and texture. If you must substitute, use full-fat coconut milk for a different version. Use a cinnamon stick -- except for a dash on the top when finished.

Use sea salt. Add the sugar slowly and taste. Make it slowly - don't be in a rush. Add the milk little by little and stir, stir, stir! This will make it super creamy.

STRAWBERRY MOUSSE

Prep Time: 10 mins
Cooking Time: 1 hr
Total Time: 10 mins
Servings: 4 servings

Ingredients

- 3/4 pound strawberries
- 1/2 cup granulated sugar
- 1 cup cold whole or whipping cream
- extra strawberries for topping

Directions

Strawberries must be cleaned and cut into slices before being combined with sugar and made into a puree in a food processor. Take out and put aside half a cup of the purée. The cream must be added to a refreshing dish and whisked until firm peaks form. After that, delicately fold in the leftover puree (not the 1/2 cup). Place the strawberry mousse on top of the 1/2 cup of puree divided among the four small or medium glasses—place in the refrigerator for about an hour or overnight if preferred. Serve the dish with sliced fresh strawberries on top.

Notes

Whipping the cream until soft peaks form may help those who want to use it as a filling. Next, add one tablespoon of water to a small pot and sprinkle the teaspoon of gelatin. Let stand for one minute, then put the pot on low flame and heat just until the gelatin has dissolved, whisking until smooth, do not boil, then immediately remove from heat.
Pour the gelatine into the cream and continue beating until firm peaks form. If the gelatine thickens too much during the reduction process, warm it again.

PERUVIAN LOMO SALTADO

Prep time: 5 mins
Cook time: 20 mins
Total time: 25 mins
Servings: 2

Ingredients

- 450g beef tenderloin, skirt steak
- 60ml peanut
- 15ml apple cider vinegar
- Two teaspoons minced fresh cilantro leaves and tender stems
- Freshly ground black pepper
- French fries for serving
- Cooked long-grain rice
- vegetable oil
- Kosher salt
- 225g red onion, cut into 1/2-inch slices
- 460g total roots and any wilted parts trimmed, remainder cut into 2-inch lengths

- 60g fresh or frozen ají amarillo chile pepper
- 160g plum tomatoes
- Two medium cloves of garlic
- 7g peeled fresh ginger
- 20ml soy sauce

Directions

Slice the beef across the grain into roughly 1/2-inch-thick strips. Heat 30ml of oil in a wok or a stainless steel pan until it is hotly smoking. Meanwhile, season beef all over with salt.
Enough beef must be added to the pan in stages so it may be seared well without losing its juices. Spread the beef out so that each piece is equally spaced apart, and cook for 30 to 1 minute until one side is nicely seared and blackened. Stir and toss the beef for around 30 seconds longer to ensure even cooking. If you're working over a gas flame and aren't nervous about a bit of fire, throw the steak close to the flame so the oil temporarily combusts in large bursts.

Transfer the meat to a dish to rest using a spatula. Repeat with remaining beef, always getting the pan smoking hot before the next batch and adding more oil if needed.

Put the empty pan back over high heat when the steak is fully cooked. Add 15ml oil and heat until smoking. Add enough red onion in small batches to cook for around 30 seconds without steaming.
Until the onion is crisp-tender, toss a few times. Transfer the onion to a plate using a spatula. Then, repeat the process with the remaining onion, making sure to heat the pan to smoking before adding any additional oil if required.

Then, add 15 cc of oil, and heat the pan on high until smoking. Scallions must be added in batches and cooked for about 30 seconds on the bottom side without stirring. Add peppers and push scallions to the side. Cook for another 30 seconds or until blackened.
Scallions and peppers are pushed to the side, tomatoes are added, and they are given a 30-second sear on one side. The tomatoes

should maintain their form rather than turning too brown and getting mushy; try not to let them become too soft and pulpy.

For about 15 seconds, while continually tossing and swirling, saute the garlic and ginger until they are gently sautéed and aromatic. Toss in the vinegar and soy sauce after adding them.

Red onions and the remaining juices from the steak should be added to the pan. Add cilantro. Add salt and pepper and toss thoroughly over high heat to mix. Get rid of the heat.
Serve the stir-fry immediately, accompanied by a heap of cooked rice and French fries.

Aj amarillo peppers have a delicious, flowery flavor and an essential dose of heat. Good Latin supermarkets frequently have frozen whole ones in the freezer area if you can't find any fresh ones. You may also substitute red bell pepper and jalapenos for a comparable amount.

GUAVA BBQ SAUCE

Prep Time:5 mins
Cook Time: 10 mins
Total Time: 15 mins
Servings: 2

Ingredients

- 1 cup guava paste cut into cubes
- 1/3 cup apple cider vinegar
- One clove of garlic minced
- 1/4 cup water
- 1/4 cup spiced rum
- Three tablespoons of tomato paste
- Three tablespoons of lime juice
- One tablespoon of soy sauce
- One tablespoon of Worcestershire sauce
- One teaspoon of liquid smoke
- Salt and pepper to taste

Directions

Combine the tomato paste, guava paste, vinegar, rum, lime juice, soy sauce, Worcestershire sauce, liquid smoke, garlic, water, salt, and pepper in a sizeable saucepan, up to a boil.

After boiling, lower the temperature to a simmer. Stirring periodically, cover and simmer for 10 to 15 minutes or until reduced. By this time, the sauce ought to be thick but pourable. After entirely cooling, transfer the sauce to a jar and refrigerate.

Notes

Guava BBQ sauce can be ready and kept in the refrigerator in an airtight container for up to two weeks.

PERUVIAN RICE PUDDING

Prep Time: 25mins
Cook Time: 2hours
Total Time: 2 hrs 25mins
Servings: 8

Ingredients

- ¼ cup coconut
- 1 cup water
- One egg yolk
- One teaspoon vanilla
- Ground cinnamon
- ¾ cup uncooked regular long-grain white rice
- 2 ½ cups whole milk
- ¼ cup sugar
- ½ cinnamon stick (about 1 1/2 inches)
- Three whole cloves
- ¼ cup raisins
- 2/3 cup sweetened condensed milk
- One piece of orange peel

Directions

In a 1-quart saucepan, heat coconut and 1 cup water over medium-high heat to boiling; boil for 10 minutes.
Meanwhile, place rice in a 2-quart saucepan; add enough cold water to cover the rice. Soak for 10 minutes. Drain; return the rice to the saucepan.

Stir in coconut and water, whole milk, sugar, cinnamon stick, and cloves. Heat to boiling on medium heat, stirring frequently. Stir in raisins. Lessen the heat; cover and simmer for about 40 minutes, stirring frequently, until rice is tender.

Stir in sweetened condensed milk and the orange peel. Cover; cook over low heat for about 10 minutes, stirring frequently, until desired consistency. Remove from heat; remove the cinnamon stick, cloves, and orange peel.

Slowly stir in egg yolk until well blended. Heat to boiling over low heat, stirring frequently. Stir in vanilla.
Place into a serving bowl. Cool slightly, about 30 minutes. Cover; refrigerate for at least 1 hour. Just before serving, sprinkle with cinnamon.

PERUVIAN CHICHA MORADA

Prep Time: 10 mins
Cook Time: 50 mins
Additional Time: 4 hrs
Total Time: 5 hrs

Ingredients

- 1-gallon water
- 15-ounce dried purple corn
- Five large lemons, juiced
- 1 ½ cups brown sugar
- ½ cup fresh pineapple, chopped
- ½ apple chopped

- Two cinnamon sticks
- One tablespoon of whole cloves

Directions

Combine the corn, cinnamon sticks, and cloves in a large pot. Carry the water to a boil, then stir in the mixture. Turn the flame down to medium-low, and simmer for forty minutes. Separate from the heat and, using a mesh strainer, separate the corn and spices from the mixture before serving.

The sugar must have completely dissolved after being mixed into the chicha and lemon juice. Refrigerate until cool. Before pouring over ice, stir in the diced pineapple and apple and then set aside.

ROAST CHICKEN-POLLO A LA BRASA

Prep Time: 15 mins
Cook Time: 1 hr
Total Time: 1 hr 15 mins
Servings: 6

Ingredients
- 2-3 pounds broiler/fryer chicken

For the marinade:
- Two tablespoons of soy sauce
- Juice of 2 limes
- 1/2 teaspoon freshly ground black pepper
- 1/2 teaspoon cayenne pepper
- Five cloves garlic
- One teaspoon of fresh ginger
- 1/4 cup dark beer
- One tablespoon of extra virgin olive oil
- One teaspoon of balsamic vinegar
- One tablespoon of huacatay paste
- One tablespoon aji panca paste

- 1 1/2 teaspoons ground cumin
- 3/4 teaspoon ground annatto
- One teaspoon of dried oregano
- One teaspoon of dried rosemary
- One teaspoon salt
- Aji Verde Sauce

Directions

Combine all the marinade components in a blender until completely smooth. Loosen the chicken's skin, then spread some marinade below. Pour the marinade over the chicken or chicken pieces in a large zipper bag. To evenly coat the pieces, swish about. Marinate overnight or for at least six hours.

If you're using a convection oven, preheat it to 470-480 degrees F and roast the chicken for 10 minutes. Roast the chicken for 15 to 20 mins, or up to the internal temperature reaches 165 degrees F, with the heat reduced to 325 degrees F.

If you're using a standard oven, preheat it to 425 degrees F, then roast the chicken pieces on the center rack for about 45 mins or up until the internal temperature of the chicken reaches 150-160 degrees F. Move the roasting pan to the lower rack if the skin starts to brown too much. The oven's temperature can also be lowered. Chicken should be taken out of the oven. Before serving, tenting the chicken with foil for 10 to 15 minutes is advised. Cut the chicken into serving pieces if you're using a whole bird.
Our homemade aji verde sauce must be served with the chicken. A lush green salad and thickly sliced French fries are common accompaniments.

Notes

The oven-roasting instructions are for chicken pieces. Increase the cooking time using a whole chicken up to the internal temperature reaches 160 degrees F.

CHICKEN BOWL WITH POTATOES

Prep time: 5 mins
Cook time: 15 mins
Total Time: 20 mins
Servings: 8

Ingredients

- 20 to 30 oz package of frozen breaded popcorn chicken
- 24 oz packages Bob Evans Original Mashed Potatoes
- 1 cup beef gravy
- 14.5 oz can whole kernel corn
- 1 cup shredded Colby-jack cheese

Direction

To make the frozen popcorn chicken extra crispy, prepare it as directed on the container, preferably in the oven or air fryer.
In the meantime, reheat the canned corn over medium heat in a tiny saucepan. Divide the Bob Evans Original Mashed Potatoes into four bowls after heating them per the package's directions.

Additionally, reheat the beef gravy per the directions on the package.

Add some crispy chicken strips, 14 cups of shredded cheese, and 13 cups of drained corn to the steaming mashed potatoes as a finishing touch. Pour the hot beef gravy over the bowl's top.

CAUSA RELLENA

Prep Time: 30mins
Cook Time: 1hr
Total Time: 1hr 30mins
Servings: 10

Ingredients

- lb Yukon Gold potatoes, cooked and peeled
- ¼ cup fresh lime juice
- One teaspoon salt
- ½ teaspoon freshly ground pepper
- Two tablespoons Peruvian yellow chiles (aji amarillo), cooked,
- mashed
- 2 cups shredded cooked chicken breast
- ½ cup frozen sweet peas, cooked
- 3/4 cup carrots, peeled
- Two tablespoons finely chopped red onion
- Two tablespoons mayonnaise

Garnish

- One tablespoon of chopped fresh parsley
- ½ cup kalamata olives
- Two hard-cooked eggs peeled
- Bibb lettuce leaves

Directions

Use a potato ricer to press potatoes or mash them until smooth. Combine potatoes, lime juice, salt, pepper, and chilies in a large bowl.

Mix the chicken, peas, carrots, onion, and mayonnaise in a medium bowl.Place half the potato mixture on a large serving dish and shape it into an 11 by 7-inch rectangle. In a dish, spoon the chicken mixture over the potato mixture—season with more salt and pepper to taste.

Shape the remaining potato mixture into a rectangle and place on top. Before serving, chill for one hour. Add parsley, olives, and chopped eggs as a garnish to the top of the potato mixture. Around the potato mixture, arrange the lettuce leaves. Square them up.

FRIED STUFFED POTATOES

Prep Time: 1 hrs
Cook Time: 45 mins
Additional Time: 2 hrs 30 mins
Total Time: 4 hrs 15 mins

Ingredients

- Four large potatoes, peeled and cubed
- 1 ½ teaspoons salt, divided
- 2 cups dry bread crumbs
- 1 cup all-purpose flour
- One tablespoon of vegetable oil
- One green bell pepper, chopped
- ½ cup chopped onion
- Three cloves garlic, minced
- 1 pound ground beef
- Four teaspoons of tomato paste
- One tablespoon of distilled white vinegar
- Two teaspoons of ground cumin
- One teaspoon of ground black pepper
- Four large eggs
- One-quarter vegetable oil

Directions

Put the potatoes in a big saucepan and add the salted water. Heat to a boil over high heat, then lower to a simmer, cover, and simmer for 20 minutes or until the vegetables are soft. Drain and let steam dry for a minute or two. Mash potatoes with 1/2 teaspoon salt in a bowl until no lumps are visible. After cooling to room temperature, place aside.

Meanwhile, heat the whole vegetable oil in a large pan over medium heat. In a heated skillet, stir green pepper, onion, and garlic for approximately 10 minutes or until the onion is tender and translucent. Turn the heat up to medium-high and add the ground meat. Cook and stir the meat until it is pink no more and crumbly.

Once the tomato paste has dissolved, add the vinegar, cumin, one teaspoon salt, and pepper. Place the beef mixture in a bowl and let it cool to room temperature.

Wax paper or plastic wrap must line a baking sheet; keep it aside. Beat eggs in a sizable bowl; set aside. Put flour and bread crumbs in separate, shallow plates and leave aside. Take a handful of mashed potatoes and divide them into two halves. Fill each piece with the meat mixture after forming it into a tiny bowl shape. To form a ball, place the pieces together, seal the edges, and smooth. With the remaining potatoes and meat mixture, repeat the same procedure.

Gently coat each potato ball in flour, one at a time; stroke off extra. Roll in bread crumbs after dipping in beaten egg. To ensure that all bread crumbs fall off, gently toss them in your hands. Put the breaded potato balls on the baking sheet that has been prepared. Either freeze for later use or refrigerate for between two and four hours.

The desired temperature is 350° F (175° C) of oil in a deep fryer or big saucepan.

Cook potato balls until crispy and golden brown in heated oil in batches, about 3 minutes for each batch, rolling the balls around as they cook for even frying.

PERUVIAN GRILLED CHICKEN

Prep Time:10 mins
Cook Time: 85 mins
Total Time: 95 mins
Servings: 4

Ingredients

- 11.6 to 1.8kg chicken
- 12g kosher salt
- 30ml vegetable or canola oil
- 18g ground cumin
- 18g paprika
- 3g freshly ground black pepper
- Three medium cloves of garlic
- 30ml white vinegar

Directions

Place the chicken breast on a large cutting board after patting it dry with paper towels. Cut down either side of the backbone with sharp kitchen shears to remove it. Lay the chicken out flat after turning it over. To flatten a chicken breast, press hard.

Run a wooden skewer horizontally through the chicken, passing through one thigh, both breast halves, and the other thigh for further support. Rearrange the wing tips. Use your fingertips to thoroughly blend the salt, cumin, garlic, vinegar, paprika, pepper, and oil in a small bowl. Spread the mixture evenly throughout the chicken's surface.

Charcoal in a chimney should be lit. Pour out and scatter the coals evenly over half of the coal grate once all the charcoal has been ignited and covered with gray ash. Alternately, turn half of a gas grill's burners to high heat. Place the cooking grate on the grill, close the lid, and let it heat up for five minutes. The grill grate has been cleaned and oiled. Place the chicken on the cooler side of the grill with the skin side up and the legs facing the hotter side. Cover the grill and position the lid's vents over the chicken. Open the grill's bottom vents.

Cook until the thickest portion of the breast registers 110°F (43°C) on an instant-read thermometer. Turn the chicken over carefully and set it skin-side down on the hotter side of the grill while orienting the breasts toward the cooler side. To ensure the chicken and grill grates make excellent contact, press down forcefully with a comprehensive, stiff spatula.

Cover the pan and continue cooking for an additional 10 minutes or until the skin is crisp and an instant-read thermometer put into the thickest section of the breast reads 145 to 150°F (63 to 66°C). If the chicken starts to burn before the desired temperature is reached, carefully move it to the cooler side of the grill, cover it, and cook it there until it is done. The chicken will burn if the lid is left off longer than necessary to monitor the temperature.

Place the chicken on a chopping board and let it a 5- to 10-minute rest. Serve with sauce after carving.

Notes

Before puréeing the jalapenos, take off the ribs and seeds for a milder sauce. Most Latin markets have aj amarillo, a yellow pepper paste from Peru. It is optional.

CHICKEN STEW

Prep Time:15 mins
Cook Time: 40 mins
Total Time: 55 mins
Servings: 6

Ingredients

- 1 ½ pounds chicken thighs
- Two tablespoons of olive oil
- 4 cups chicken broth or chicken stock
- 1 cup green beans or peas
- ½ cup heavy cream
- Two carrots diced
- One small onion
- Two stalks of celery diced
- Five tablespoons flour divided
- ½ teaspoon rosemary
- ½ teaspoon thyme
- ¼ teaspoon sage
- salt and pepper to taste
- 1 ½ cups potatoes peeled and diced
- 1 ½ cups sweet potatoes peeled and diced
- ½ red pepper finely diced
- ¼ cup white wine

Directions

Chicken must be browned in 1 tablespoon of olive oil in a sizable saucepan or Dutch oven. Take out of the pot and reserve. For about 3 minutes, or until the onion softens, cook the remaining olive oil with the onion, carrot, and celery. Add spices, three tablespoons of flour, and salt and pepper to taste. Cook for roughly 2 minutes on medium heat.

Add the browned chicken, potatoes, sweet potatoes, red pepper, white wine, and broth. Carry to a boil, lower the heat, and cover the saucepan to simmer for 30 minutes.

Remove the cover, then whisk in the cream and green beans. If desired, thicken the mixture and boil uncovered for 10 minutes.

The remaining two tablespoons of flour and 1 cup of water or broth must be combined in a mason jar to thicken. Shake vigorously, then add to the boiling stew for consistency.

BROCCOLI CHEDDAR SOUP

Prep Time: 10 mins
Cook Time: 20 mins
Total time: 30mins
Servings: 4

Ingredients

- Four tablespoons butter ½ stick
- ½ medium onion chopped
- 2 cups light or heavy milk
- 2 cups grated cheddar cheese
- 2-3 cloves garlic
- Four tablespoon AP flour
- 2 cups low-sodium chicken or vegetable stock
- 1 tsp kosher salt
- ½ tsp black pepper
- ¼ tsp paprika or ground nutmeg
- 3 cups broccoli florets
- One large carrot grated

Directions

Omelt the whole butter in a big saucepan or Dutch oven on medium-high heat. When the onion is soft and light gold, add it and cook for 3 to 4 minutes. Sauté for another minute after adding the garlic. Include the flour and stir for 1 to 2 mins or until the flour turns golden. Add the spices, broccoli florets, carrots, and chicken stock. Carry to a boil, lower the heat to a simmer, cover, and cook for 12-15 mins or up until the broccoli and carrots are tender.

Add the cheddar cheese and half & half, then simmer for one more minute. If necessary, taste and adjust the seasoning.

MUSHROOM & POTATO SOUP

Prep Time: 15 mins
Cook Time: 30 mins
Total Time: 45mins
Servings: 4

Ingredients

- 1 tbsp rapeseed oil
- Two large onions
- 8 tbsp bio yogurt
- 55g walnut pieces
- 20g dried porcini mushrooms
- 3 tsp vegetable bouillon powder
- 300g chestnut mushrooms, chopped
- Three garlic cloves
- 300g potato, finely diced
- 2 tsp fresh thyme
- Four carrots
- 2 tbsp chopped parsley

Directions

In a big pan, the oil is heating. Include the onions and cook them for 10 mins or until golden. In the meantime, add the bouillon and 1.2 liters of boiling water to the dried mushrooms.

Add the fresh mushrooms, garlic, thyme, potatoes, and carrots, and cook until the mushrooms soften and brown.
Stock and dried mushrooms should be added. Cover the pan and boil for 20 mins. Add lots of pepper and parsley after mixing.

Pour into meals and top with two tablespoons of yogurt and a quarter of the walnuts for each serving. You may refrigerate the leftovers and reheat them the following day.

CHUPE DE QUINOA PERUVIAN SOUP

Prep Time: 20 minutes
Cook Time: 30 minutes
Servings: 6 to 8 servings

Ingredients

Fried Fish:
- Six pieces of cod
- 1/2 cup flour
- One tablespoon of olive oil
- 1/2 teaspoon salt
- 1/2 teaspoon black pepper

Soup:
- 1 cup cubed squash
- 1/2 cup peas
- 1 cup Clamato Tomato Cocktail
- One can evaporate milk
- 6 to 8 eggs (1 egg per person)
- 1 cup queso fresco cut into chunks
- 1 French baguette
- One tablespoon butter
- 1/2 cup lima beans
- 1 cup corn
- 1 cup diced carrots
- Four yellow potatoes cubed
- Two tablespoons of olive oil
- One small red onion
- Two garlic cloves minced

- Two tablespoons minced mint
- One tablespoon of dried oregano
- Two teaspoons salt
- One teaspoon of ground pepper
- Two tablespoons ají amarillo
- 4 cups fish stock

Directions

Fish:
1. Pat the fish dry on all sides using paper towels.
2. combine the salt, flour, and pepper on a plate.
3. Shake strongly to remove extra flour after coating the fish on all sides and pressing down firmly to ensure it sticks.

Two pieces of fish must be cooked at a time in hot olive oil over medium heat. Cook for 2 minutes, carefully pushing down until brown and crisp, then turn. After 2 minutes of crisp cooking on the opposite side, remove. Place aside.

Vegetables:

Fill a saucepan with water, then add the squash, peas, lima beans, corn, carrots, and potatoes. Carry to a boil and cook for 10 mins or until potatoes are tender. This step can be completed a few days before and stored in the refrigerator.

Soup:

1. In a big saucepan, heat some oil over medium-high heat.
2. Include the onion and cook for four minutes.
3. Include the garlic and cook for one more minute.

Bring to a boil the C Tomato Cocktail and fish stock. Add salt, pepper, oregano, mint, aj amarillo, and the vegetables you set out earlier. For 10 minutes, cook. Six eggs are dropped, the heat is reduced, and evaporated milk is added. For five minutes, simmer it with the cover on.

Warm up a small frying pan, add 1/2 tablespoon of butter, and cook a couple of pieces of bread while the soup is boiling. Continue until you have enough slices for all of your visitors.

After adding bits of queso fresco, turn off the burner and serve the soup.

CHICKEN POTATO SALAD

Prep Time: 20 mins
Cook Time: 20 mins
Total Time: 40 mins

Ingredients

- Six large potatoes
- 1/2 pound chicken breast or thigh meat, boneless and skinless
- 1/4 cup sweetened condensed milk
- salt and pepper to taste
- One medium carrot peeled
- Three hard-boiled eggs peeled
- One small onion peeled
- 1 cup crushed pineapple
- 1/4 cup sweet pickle relish
- 1/2 cup ham, cubed
- 1 cup mayonnaise

Directions

Thoroughly rinse potatoes under cold running water. Put the potatoes and enough cold water to cover them in a large pot. Bring to a boil over medium heat. Potatoes must be covered and cooked for 12 to 15 mins or until soft but not falling apart.

Drain the potatoes, then let them cool. Remove and throw away skins. Cut the food into 1-inch cubes with a knife.

Put the chicken and enough water to cover it in a saucepan. After bringing the water to a boil, turn down the heat. Cook the chicken thoroughly in a simmer for 15 to 20 minutes.

Keep the chicken away from the liquid, let it cool completely, then shred it. Place aside.

Bring water to a boil in a saucepan. Cook the chopped carrots for 30 seconds after adding them. Remove from water with a slotted spoon, then put into an ice bath to chill thoroughly. Drain, then set apart. Potatoes, chicken onions, crushed pineapple, carrots, eggs, sweet pickle relish, ham, mayonnaise, and condensed milk must all be combined in a big dish. Gently combine and mix until everything is spread.

To taste, include salt and pepper in the food. Thirty minutes ought to pass in the refrigerator for the flavors to blend.

Notes

Before adding the remaining ingredients, let the potatoes cool fully since any remaining heat will melt the mayonnaise and turn the salad into an excessively oily mess. Put the potatoes on a baking sheet in a thin layer, cover, and chill to hasten cooling.

SALMON AND CRAB CEVICHE

Total Time: 1 hr 30 mins
Servings: 6

Ingredients
- 1 ½ pounds boned, skinned wild salmon
- ¾ cup lime juice
- Two medium tomatoes
- ½ red onion chopped
- ½ cup coarsely chopped cilantro
- Two tablespoons extra-virgin olive oil

- 1/4 cup pickled jalapeño
- ½ to 1 serrano chile
- One teaspoon of kosher salt
- ½ teaspoon dried oregano
- Mini (3 in.) crisp tostada shells

Directions

In a glass dish, combine the salmon and lime juice. Allow it to rest for about 30 minutes, stirring regularly, until the salmon is opaque and somewhat stiff to the touch. In the meantime, combine all the remaining components in a separate bowl except the tostada shells.
Remove all except three tablespoons of the lime juice from the fish. Salmon and tomato combination should be combined with tostada shells on the side.

In well-stocked Latino stores, you may find little tostada shells.
The 2012 "Bella Flor" Dry Rosé of Syrah from Ceja. This pink, exquisitely crisp, balances the tart citrus flavors of the ceviche, and its vibrant red fruit cools the chiles and highlights the wild salmon.

TAMALES

Prep Time: 30 mins
Cook Time: 3 hrs
Total Time: 3 hrs 30 mins

Ingredients

Chile Sauce:
- 4 dried chile peppers
- 2 cups water
- 1 ½ teaspoons salt

Filling:
- One ¼ pounds pork loin
- One large onion, halved
- One clove garlic

Husks and Dough:
- 8-ounce dried corn husks
- ⅔ cup lard
- ½ teaspoon salt
- 1 cup sour cream
- 10.5-ounce beef broth
- 2 cups masa harina
- One teaspoon of baking powder

Directions

Making the filling In a Dutch oven, combine the meat, onion, and garlic. Bring to a boil after covering with just enough water. Reduce heat to low and simmer for about two hours or until meat is well cooked.

Use gloves made of latex to remove the stems and seeds from the chilies before making the sauce. Put the chilies and two cups of water in a saucepan—twenty minutes of uncovered boiling. Please take off the heat and let it cool.

Blend the chiles and cooking liquid in a blender until smooth. The mixture should be strained into a basin and salted. Place aside. Mix 1 cup of chile sauce with 1 cup of shredded cooked pork. Save the leftover sauce for dishing.

Corn husks should be softened for around 30 minutes by soaking them in a dish of warm water. The same goes for the dough. Make fluffy lard by beating it with one tablespoon of broth while the husks are soaking. In another basin, combine the masa harina, salt, and baking soda; stir into the lard mixture.

Husks must be drained and pat dry. To a 1/4-1/2 inch thickness, spread the dough over the husks. Spread each with a teaspoon of the pork filling in the center. Each husk is folded inward from the top, bottom, and sides toward the center to contain the dough. In a steamer basket, arrange the tamales. For one hour, steam the item over a boiling pot of water. Take tamales out of their husks. Top with sour cream and drizzle with any residual chile sauce, or, for a creamier sauce, combine sour cream and chile sauce first.

Tips

Beef or chicken may be used in place of the pork.

CHICKEN SOUP WITH QUINOA

Prep Times: 20 mins
Cook times: 40 mins
Total: 1 hour
Servings: 8

Ingredients

- Two tablespoons of olive oil
- One 15-oz. can of northern beans drained and rinsed
- One tablespoon of minced garlic
- Three bay leaves
- 1/8 teaspoon ground black pepper
- One lb. boneless skinless chicken breast
- 1/4 teaspoon salt
- Two teaspoons of freshly grated ginger
- Two teaspoons of newly grated lemongrass
- Three large carrots sliced and halved
- Three large celery stalks sliced
- 1/2 medium yellow onion
- 8 cups chicken broth
- 3/4 cup uncooked quinoa
- One tablespoon of Frank's Hot Sauce
- bundle of rosemary
- One medium lemon juiced
- Fresh parsley for serving

Directions

First, prepare veggies by slicing and halving three large carrots. Then cut up a medium yellow onion and three giant celery stalks into fine pieces—heat 2 tbsp of cooking oil (olive oil) on medium in a big stockpot. Add carrots, celery, onion, grated ginger, grated lemongrass, and chopped garlic when the olive oil is aromatic. Vegetables must be sautéed for 5 to 7 minutes or until the onions are transparent.

Add the raw chicken breast, great northern beans, uncooked quinoa, spicy sauce, rosemary bundle, bay leaves, salt, and pepper afterward. Combine, then bring to a rapid boil. Once boiling, lower the heat and cover. Allow to boil for thirty minutes. Remove the rosemary bundle and throw it away when the soup simmered for 30 minutes. Shred the chicken breast with two forks after removing it. Re-add the chicken that has been shredded into the stockpot and stir.

A whole lemon's worth of lemon juice must be added after the heat has been turned off. Add some lemon wedges and fresh parsley to the dish.

Notes

Lemongrass that has been grated:

If you need help locating lemongrass that has been grated paste form, feel free to use a stick of fresh lemongrass instead. In step 4, add this, then in step 7, remove it.

Make a rosemary bundle by bundling four or five rosemary sprigs with baker's twine.

CONFETTI QUINOA

Total Time: 20mins
servings: 4-5

Ingredients

- 2 cups water
- 1 cup quinoa, rinsed
- 1/2 cup chopped fresh broccoli
- 1/2 cup coarsely chopped zucchini
- 1/4 cup shredded carrots
- 1/2 teaspoon salt
- One tablespoon of lemon juice
- One tablespoon of olive oil

Directions

Add quinoa to boiling water and salt. Lessen the heat, then cover and simmer for 15 mins until water is absorbed. Meanwhile, sauté onion and pepper in olive oil. Add to cooked quinoa; add almonds or water chestnuts just before serving.

CHICKEN AND RICE SOUP

Prep Time: 15 mins
Cook Time: 30 mins
Total Time: 45 mins
Servings: 6

Ingredients

- One tablespoon oil
- One onion minced
- 1 cup evaporated milk
- Three large carrots peeled and diced
- One stalk of celery diced
- One teaspoon garlic minced
- One teaspoon of dried parsley

- ½ teaspoon dried thyme
- One teaspoon salt
- ⅛ teaspoon black pepper
- 5 cups low-sodium chicken broth
- Two chicken breasts uncooked
- 1 cup brown rice

Directions

Oil must be heated over medium-high heat in a big soup pot. When the onion starts to golden, add the carrots and celery and cook and stiring for 3 to 4 minutes for one minute after adding the garlic, parsley, and thyme. Add chicken, broth, salt, and pepper. Put rice in. Stir and heat on medium-high, bringing to a boil.

When the veggies and rice are soft, reduce the heat to medium-low, cover the pan, and cook for 30 mins, stirring every 10 minutes. Chicken from the saucepan, then shred it. Add evaporated milk back to the saucepan.

MARINATED CHICKEN

Prep Time: 5 mins
Cook Time:10 mins
Chill Time: 30 mins
Total Time:55 mins
Servings:6

Ingredients
- ½ cup extra virgin olive oil
- 1 ½ teaspoons salt
- One teaspoon of ground black pepper
- Two teaspoons of garlic powder
- Six chicken breasts
- ½ cup balsamic vinegar or other vinegar
- ¼ cup low-sodium soy sauce
- ¼ cup Worcestershire sauce
- ⅛ cup lemon juice

- ¾ cup brown sugar
- Two teaspoons of dried rosemary
- Two tablespoons Spicy Brown mustard

Directions

Combine all marinade components in a large mixing bowl and whisk together. Half of the marinade must be taken out and saved for basting the chicken later.

Put the chicken in a large sealable bag and cover it with the marinade. Chicken breasts should be gently stroked, and the bag should be closed tightly.

Chicken must be marinated for at least 30 minutes and up to 24 hours in the refrigerator. Between 4 and 6 hours is ideal. To grill. Heat the grill to medium heat and give the grates a little oiling.Take the chicken out of the marinade and let the extra liquid drip. Cook the chicken thoroughly on the grill for 5 to 6 minutes on each side.

Use the marinade that was set aside to baste the chicken occasionally. Keep away the chicken from the grill once it reaches 165°F and tent with foil. Before serving, give the chicken at least five minutes to rest.

Notes

Grilling:
1. Heat the grill to a medium-high setting and give the grates a little oiling.
2. Take the chicken out of the marinade and let the extra liquid drip.
3. Cook the chicken thoroughly on the grill for 5 to 6 minutes on each side. The internal temperature of chicken must reach 160-165°F.
4. Use the marinade set aside to baste the chicken occasionally.
5. Take the chicken from the grill, and tent it with foil.
6. give the chicken at least five minutes to rest before serving.

Oven to 400 degrees for baking. Place the marinated chicken on a shallow baking sheet or pan, and bake for 18 to 22 minutes (or 15 to 18 minutes at 450 degrees if you're in a rush), or up to the internal temperature of the chicken reaches 165 degrees. Before serving, give the chicken at least five minutes to rest. For the finest taste, baste as frequently as you can.

ROTISSERIE TURKEY

Prep Time: 15 mins
Cook Time: 3 hrs
Total Time: 3hrs 15mins

Ingredients

- 13 pounds of turkey, fresh or frozen turkey that has wholly thawed
- One tablespoon of kosher salt
- 1 ½ teaspoons garlic pepper
- Olive oil
- paprika to cover

Directions

Preheat a gas grill to 350 degrees. Any remaining turkey bits must be taken out and thrown away. Use cold water to wash the turkey's exterior and cavity thoroughly. With a paper towel, dry. Turkey truss. (To maintain its form, poultry must be trussed or knotted before cooking.) Apply olive oil generously all over the turkey's exterior. 1 tsp of kosher salt and 3/4 teaspoon of garlic pepper should be used to season the turkey's inside.

Safely place the bird on the rotisserie. Apply the remaining kosher salt and garlic pepper to the turkey's exterior. Adjust the proportions of garlic, pepper, and kosher salt if necessary. Paprika must be liberally applied to the turkey's exterior. On the rotisserie base of the hot grill, place the turkey. Per pound, let 10-15 minutes. Refrain from base completion on an estimated time. Use a meat thermometer as a guide.

Too many factors can affect cooking time, which can affect doneness. To avoid food-borne diseases, pay attention to the interior temperature of your turkey. Internal breast and thigh temperatures must exceed 170° and 180°, respectively.

Take the turkey off the grill, then wrap it in foil. Before cutting, let the turkey 20 minutes to rest.

Notes

Remember that a turkey greater than 12 to 14 pounds won't fit in most rotisserie devices that come with grills.

EASY CHICKEN POT PIE

Prep Time: 10 mins
Total Time: 45 mins
Servings: 6

Ingredients

- 1 1/2 cups frozen mixed vegetables
- 1 cup chopped cooked chicken
- One tablespoon of vegetable oil
- One egg
- 10 ½ ozc ondensed cream of chicken soup
- 1 cup Bisquick™ Original Pancake & Baking Mix
- ½ cup milk

Directions

Keep the heat in the oven to 375 degrees. Spray cooking oil in a 9-inch pie pan. Stir in the soup, chicken, and vegetables.Mix the remaining components in a medium bowl. Pour into the pie dish. Bake for 29 to 33 minutes, uncovered, or until the crust is a deep golden brown.

PASTEL DE PAPAS

Prep Time: 35 mins
Cook Time: 1 hrs 5 mins
Additional Time: 10 mins
Total Time: 1 hrs 50 mins

Ingredients

- 5 cups potatoes, peeled and cubed
- Two tablespoons of buttersalt to taste
- One pinch of cayenne pepper
- salt and black pepper to taste
- Two large eggs, beaten
- ½ cup vegetable oil
- One medium onion
- One clove of garlic, minced
- Two medium tomatoes
- One tablespoon of tomato paste
- 1 pound ground beef
- Two tablespoons shredded Panquehue cheese
- ½ teaspoon chopped fresh parsley

Directions

Put the potatoes in a big saucepan, add salted water, and boil. After about 20 minutes of simmering, lower the heat to medium-low.
Oil must be heated in a big pan over medium heat while the potatoes cook.

Add the onion; cook and stir for approximately 5 minutes or until it becomes translucent. Add the garlic at the last minute. Cook for 3-5 mins, stirring occasionally, until tomatoes soften and start to lose their structure. Include the ground beef in the skillet and cook, stirring for 8-10 mins or until browned and crumbly. Add cayenne pepper, parsley, and Panquehue cheese after seasoning with salt and pepper. Let the heat be turned off and sit until required. The oven must be heated at 350 degrees F (175 degrees C). In a 2-quart baking dish, grease it.

Potatoes must be drained in a strainer and steam-dried for one to two minutes. Return the potatoes to the saucepan, season with salt and butter, and mash until smooth. Stir in the beaten egg after cooling it for 5-0 mins until warm.

In the bottom of the baking dish that has been prepared, spread 1/2 of the mashed potatoes. The leftover potatoes should be thoroughly layered on the ground beef mixture.
Bake in the oven for about 40 minutes or until the potatoes are hot and the tops are gently browned.

STEAK BITES AND POTATOES

Prep Time: 10 mins
Cook Time: 20 mins
Total Time: 30 mins
Servings: 4

Ingredients

- 1 pound beef steak. Any cut will work
- Sprinkle of salt
- Two tablespoons water
- A sprinkle of black pepper.
- Three tablespoons of sesame oil
- Three red potatoes – diced
- 1 cup water
- One large red bell pepper
- One white onion – sliced into strips
- One tablespoon garlic – minced
- ½ teaspoon ground ginger
- 1 cup mushrooms – optional
- 2/3 cup water
- 1/4 cup soy sauce

- Two tablespoons cornstarch

Directions

Add enough salt and black or Szechuan pepper to the meat before serving—3 tablespoons sesame oil and high heat in a pan or wok.
Steak must be seared for about two minutes on each side; then, it should be removed from the fire and rest. Add potatoes and a cup of water to the pan or wok while the steak rests.

Cook for about 7 minutes until potato pieces soften; test for doneness by piercing one with a fork; they don't have to be entirely soft now.

If using mushrooms, add them now as well. Cook the potatoes for about 2 minutes or until the onions, peppers, and mushrooms soften. Stir in the ginger and garlic.

While chopping the steak, add the water and soy sauce and mix for one or two minutes until everything is thoroughly combined. After cutting the steak into bite-sized pieces, add it to the pan or wok.

Combine all of the ingredients. Combine the cornstarch and water in a separate small meal, then immediately pour and swirl the mixture into the stir fry.
Remove the stir-fry sauce from the heat as it starts to thicken. If preferred, include salt and pepper to taste. Serve with stir-fried rice or noodles or over rice.

SWEET POTATO & CAULIFLOWER LENTIL BOWL

Prep Times: 20 mins
Cook Times: 35 mins
Servings: 4

Ingredients

- One large sweet potato, slice into medium chunks
- One cauliflower, cut into large florets
- Two carrots
- ¼ red cabbage
- ½ small pack of coriander
- 1 tbsp garam masala
- 3 tbsp groundnut oil
- Two garlic cloves
- 200g puy lentils
- a thumb-sized piece of ginger, grated
- 1 tsp Dijon mustard
- 1½ limes, juiced

Directions

The oven must be heated to 200°C/180°F/gas 6. Combine the garam masala, half the oil, and some spice with the sweet potato and cauliflower. On a large roasting tray, spread out. Roast the garlic for 30-35 minutes or until cooked.

In the meantime, combine the lentils with 400 ml of cool water in a saucepan. When the lentils are done but still have some bite, simmer for 20–25 minutes after bringing them to a boil. Drain.

Cut the garlic cloves from the tray and crush them with your knife's edge. Combine the garlic, remaining oil, ginger, mustard, a sprinkle of sugar, and one-third of the lime juice in a large bowl. Add the heated lentils after whisking, toss them, and then season to taste. Grate the carrots coarsely, shred the cabbage, and cut the coriander roughly.

Include the rest of the lime juice and season to taste. The lentil mixture should be divided into four meals. Include a quarter of the sweet potato, cauliflower combination, and carrot slaw on each surface.

PANCAKES HUANCAINA

Prep Time: 15 mins
Cook Time: 35 mins
Total Time: 50 mins
Servings: 4

Ingredients

- 1 cup Salsa Huancaina chilled
- One egg slightly whipped
- a large pinch of Kosher salt
- Two ¾ cups milk divided
- 1 cup masa harina
- 1 cup flour
- One tablespoon of baking powder

Directions

In a sizable mixing bowl, combine a cup of cold Salsa Huancaina, one egg, and a cup of milk. Blend by stirring, but wait to whip too quickly. Avoid adding excessive amounts of air to the mixture.

Mix the masa harina, flour, baking soda, and salt in a separate basin. Add the dry ingredients to the cheese, egg, and cheese mixture while whisking it gently. The wet components should be combined with the dry ones to prevent lumps from developing.

When the mixture has thick pancake batter consistency, thin it out by adding additional milk while stirring.
Let the batter sit in the refrigerator for about 15 minutes to moisten all the dry ingredients thoroughly. They must add some extra milk because the batter stiffens slightly while resting.

For around 5 to 10 minutes, heat a griddle or skillet with a heavy bottom over medium heat. A surface temperature of about 350 degrees is ideal. You may check if it is sufficient by sprinkling water on the surface. It's too cold if it sits there and steams but too hot if it vanishes immediately. When the water "dances" before dissipating, you will know the surface is the ideal temperature for cooking.
Apply cooking spray to the cooking surface.

1/4 cup of pancake batter should be poured onto the pan. Ensure at least a quarter-inch of space between each pancake when cooking numerous pancakes simultaneously.
For two to three minutes, don't touch the pancake. You should notice little bubbles bursting on the pancakes, and the edges will start to dry out. Cook for a further two to three minutes after flipping the pancakes.

Serve right away or keep warm in a low oven covered with foil.

HUMITAS OR STEAMED FRESH CORN CAKES

Prep Time: 1 hr
Cook time: 40 mins
Total Time: 1 hrs 40 mins
Servings: 12–15

Ingredients

- 4–5 corn cobs
- 2–3 garlic cloves
- ¼ tsp pepper
- 230 g goat's feta, white sheep's milk cheese, or cream cheese
- 125 ml evaporated milk
- 250 g pre-cooked cornmeal
- 2 tsp baking powder
- One medium bunch of coriander, chopped
- 200 g lard
- Two medium-large red onions, chopped
- 2 tsp ground cumin

- ¼ cup chili paste
- 1 tsp salt

Directions

The corn cobs' husks should be removed and preserved. Take out and throw away the silks. Corn husks should be cooked in boiling water for 5 minutes. Slice the corn kernels from the cobs while waiting. For this meal, 500 g of kernels are required. Mix the corn kernels, garlic, and evaporated milk until smooth. Add the cornmeal, baking soda, and coriander to the bowl.

In a large frying pan, melt the fat. The onion must have softened. Cook for 2–3 minutes after adding the cumin and aji paste. Add the corn mixture after seasoning with salt and pepper, and cook for 3-4 mins. Add the cheese after removing from the heat and letting it cool somewhat. Continue to stand until cool.

Two corn husks are flat, slightly overlapping on a work surface, with the more prominent edges parallel. On the husks, spread 2 to 3 tbsp of the corn mixture.
Over the corn mixture, fold the husk on one side. Husks are wrapped by folding the opposite side over and tucked in the sharp end. Some softened husks may be torn into tiny strips to tie humitas.

Humitas must be placed in a steamer, and they should steam for 20 to 25 minutes, adding water as needed to keep the pot from boiling dry. Cool a little before serving.

Notes

Conventional oven temperatures must be 20 C lower when using fan-forced (convection) ovens. | Our cups and tablespoons are Australian units: One tablespoon is equivalent to 20 milliliters, of one cup is equal to 250 milliliters. | All veggies are medium size and peeled unless indicated. | All eggs are 55-60 gm unless specified. | All herbs are fresh (unless stated), and cups are gently packed.

LAMB SHANKS

Prep Time:10 mins
Cook Time: 2 hrs 50 mins
Total Time: 3 hrs
Servings: 4

Ingredients

- 350 - 400g lamb shanks
- ½ tsp cooking salt
- Two bay leaves
- Sauce thickener
- 6 tsp cornflour
- 2 tbsp water
- 30 g / 2 tbsp cold unsalted butter
- 1 tsp black pepper
- 3 tbsp olive oil
- Three garlic cloves minced
- 2 tbsp tomato paste
- 1 liter beef stock/broth
- 1 cup water
- Red wine marinade
- One small onion
- One small carrot
- One celery stem
- 750 ml pinot noir, red wine
- 2 tsp dried thyme

To Serve:
- Mashed potato, polenta, or pureed cauliflower
- Finely chopped fresh parsley or thyme leaves

Directions

Lamb shanks should be marinated for 24 hours. Combine the red wine marinade ingredients in a dish or other container. As much as possible, arrange the legs so the meat is buried in the wine.
Cover the bowl and marinate for 24 hrs in the refrigerator. Set the oven to 160 °C. Reduce wine: Pour the red wine (leaving the shanks, vegetables, and herbs in the filter) into a big pot. Over medium-high heat, quickly simmer for a few minutes until reduced by half. The scum that rises to the surface should be scooped off and discarded.

Shanks are seared; use paper towels to pat them dry. After that, season with salt and pepper. Heat two tbsp of oil over high heat in a large saucepan with a sturdy base. Two shanks at a time, sear until evenly browned, about 5 minutes. Repeat after removing to a platter.

Aromatic ingredients should be sautéed. Drain and skim off any extra fat. Medium low on the stove. Warm up the final tablespoon of oil. Add the garlic along with the colander's wine-stained veggies and herbs. For five minutes, cook. Cook for two minutes after adding the tomato paste.

Red wine reduction, stock, and water are added to the boiling liquid while stirring. Lamb shanks should be added to the drink and arranged as best you can so the meaty ends are immersed. If they aren't completely submerged, don't panic; they will shrink while cooking and sink to the bottom of the liquid, and exposed portions will still steam-cook.

Turn raise the heat on the stove and simmer the liquid to slow-cook it. The beef should be fork-tender and clinging to the bone when covered and placed in the oven for 2 Horus 20 minutes. For other cooking techniques, see the notes.

Remove the lamb shanks to a platter from the pot. To stay warm, loosely cover with foil.

Restaurant presentation:

Tightly wrap the shank meat in plastic wrap, then press it down the bone to produce a tidy shape. As they gently cool, the shanks will maintain their shape, so keep them covered while you prepare the sauce.

The sauce should be reduced; do not push the vegetable juices out of the sauce when you strain it into a dish. Return the sauce to the saucepan and boil it for 10-15 mins over medium heat to reduce it to 2 cups. Keep an eye on it toward the end since it decreases quickly!

Cornflour and water should be combined, then added to the sauce to thicken it. 2 minutes of simmering is sufficient to achieve a thin syrupy consistency. Keep the saucepan away from the burner and add butter to it. The sauce will thicken more as you stir the melted butter in.

Final season:

Taste the sauce and, if necessary, season with extra salt. You shouldn't need any extra if using low-sodium stock from a shop. You'll need an additional 1/4 to 1/2 tsp of salt using my beef stock.

Notes

Ensure you get lamb shanks that fit in your cooking pot because sizes vary widely. I use a 26 cm/11" diameter Chasseur Dutch oven, which comfortably accommodates 4 x 400g/13oz lamb shanks. It suffices if the meaty end is mostly immersed; they don't need to be entirely buried.

If your pot isn't big enough, use a baking dish for the slow-cooking portion instead. If the baking dish has no lid, cover it with two layers of foil.

ARROZ CON POLLO

Prep Time: 15 mins
Cook Time: 1 hr
Total Time: 1 hrs 15 mins
Servings: 4 to 6

Ingredients

- 2¾ teaspoons salt
- ¼ teaspoon ground black pepper
- ¼ tsp ground turmeric
- ½ teaspoon sugar
- ¾ cup drained and halved pimento-stuffed green olives (from a 6-oz jar)
- Two bay leaves
- 1 cup frozen peas, thawed
- ¼ cup chopped fresh cilantro
- Lemon or lime wedges
- Two teaspoons of ground cumin
- Three ib bone-in, skin-on chicken thighs, and drumsticks
- Two tablespoons of vegetable oil
- One medium yellow onion, chopped
- One medium green bell pepper, chopped
- 2 cups long-grain white rice
- Six cloves garlic, minced
- ¼ cup tomato paste
- 3½ cups chicken broth
- ½ teaspoon dried oregano

Directions

Set an oven rack in the middle and heat the oven to 350°F. Mix 1½ teaspoons of salt, pepper, and one teaspoon of cumin in a small bowl.

Remove any extra chicken fat by trimming it off. Make sure all sides of the chicken are dry before seasoning.

On medium-high heat, warm the oil in a large Dutch oven or heavy pan that can be used in the range. Brown the chicken in two batches to avoid overcrowding the pan. For thighs, arrange the chicken skin side down and fry for 5 to 7 minutes or until golden and crisp. Flip, and brown the other side for one to two minutes longer.

Drumsticks must be seared on each side for two to three minutes, flipping for equal browning. Transfer the chicken to a large platter and put aside using tongs. Pour out all but roughly two tablespoons of the fat if a lot of oil is still in the pan.

Put the skillet back on the flame and lower the temperature to medium-low. Add the bell pepper and onion, and simmer for 6 to 8 minutes while stirring periodically until the vegetables are soft. Any browned parts at the bottom of the pan should be scraped off and combined with the vegetables as you stir. Cook the rice, tomato paste, remaining one teaspoon of cumin, and garlic for 2 to 3 more minutes, stirring regularly, until fragrant.

Add 114 teaspoons of salt, oregano, turmeric, sugar, olives, bay leaves, and chicken broth. Pour any leftover chicken drippings into the pan and nestle the chicken on top of this mixture. Bring to a boil, then immediately transfer the pot to the oven, where it will bake for 35 mins, or until the chicken reaches 175°F on a meat thermometer. The pan must be removed from the oven and left to cool for ten minutes while covered on a wire rack or stovetop.

To move the chicken to a platter, remove the lid from the pan. Flake the rice after removing the bay leaves. Make sure the rice is thoroughly cooked by giving it a taste. Rice should be combined with peas and cilantro. Add the chicken pieces back to the rice's surface. Alternatively, remove the meat, pull it off the bones, shred it into bite-sized pieces, and combine it with the rice. When ready to serve, cover the pan to keep it warm for 30 minutes. Serve with slices of lemon or lime.

PICKLED CUCUMBERS AND ONION

Prep Time: 10 mins
Inactive: 5 hrs
Cook Time: 10 mins
Total Time: 5 hrs 20 mins
Servings: 3 to 4

Ingredients

- 1 hothouse seedless cucumber
- ½ small red onion
- 5 to 6 allspice berries
- ¼ teaspoon kosher salt
- Two tablespoons fresh picked dill sprigs
- 1 ½ cups white vinegar
- 1 cup sugar

Directions

Finely slice the cucumbers and red onion using a mandoline or a sharp knife. Place in a mixing dish with the dill sprigs and some salt as you prepare the pickling solution.

Salt, allspice, sugar, and white vinegar are mixed and heated in a small saucepan over medium heat. Stir the mixture thoroughly after it has reached a simmer and the sugar has dissolved. Pickling liquid is poured over the red onion and cucumbers; mix to coat thoroughly. After allowing it to reach room temperature, wrap it in plastic and place it in the refrigerator.

Ensure it has chilled in the fridge for at least 4 hours before serving.

PERUVIAN POTATO SALAD

Total Time: 50 mins

servings: 4

Ingredients

- ½ an onion
- Six tablespoons yellow pepper paste
- ½ cup of black olives
- ½ a lime
- Chopped fresh parsley
- Salt
- 250g queso fresco
- ¼ to 1/3 cup olive oil
- ½ cup evaporated milk or whole milk
- 3-4 water crackers or saltines
- Four eggs, hard-boiled
- 2 pounds assorted small potatoes

Directions

Two teaspoons of olive oil must be used to sauté the onion in a pan over medium heat until it begins to become brown. Cook the pepper paste for one minute while stirring. Use an immersion blender in the pan or move the contents to a blender.

Add milk, crackers, queso fresco, salt, pepper, and 1/4 cup olive oil. Until smooth, blend. Include lime juice, taste, and adjust seasoning as needed. If you want a thinner consistency, stir in the remaining olive oil.

In the meanwhile, boil potatoes in a big pot of salted water. Drain, add a few tablespoons of olive oil and the lime juice to a large bowl, stir, and cool. If you prefer a cold salad, you may prepare the potatoes and the eggs in advance. Place the potatoes and a component of the pepper sauce on a serving platter.

Place additional sauce on top, top with parsley, then place the quartered eggs around the bowl's perimeter. If used, scatter the olives on top. If wanted, serve with an item of additional sauce that has been drizzled with olive oil.

Notes

If you can get little potatoes, use those. They are more rigidly built. But you may still use the potatoes you usually use to make your favorite potato salad.

You might prepare a batch and store it in the refrigerator. Described below is a handmade recipe. If you need help finding Peruvian yellow peppers, you may also get aji amarillo sauce online.

Although they are not precisely the same, you can substitute the queso fresco with a mixture of hard ricotta, some cream cheese, and a combination of ordinary yellow pepper and habanero peppers.

BEEF EMPANADAS

Prep Time: 5 mins
Cook Time: 25 mins
Total Time:30mins
Servings: 4

Ingredients

- ½ pound ground beef
- ¼ onion diced
- ½ teaspoon ground cumin
- ½ teaspoon chili powder or chipotle chili powder
- ½ teaspoon salt
- 4 ounces diced green chiles
- 4 ounces diced pimento peppers
- Two tablespoons of tomato paste
- ½ cup shredded sharp cheddar cheese

- Two refrigerated pie crusts
- One egg whisked

Directions

The oven temperature should be between 380 and 400 degrees. Use a nonstick mat to line a baking sheet. Pie crusts must be unrolled on a clean, level surface. Cut circles from the dough using a 3-inch round pastry cutter. The ground beef should be browned over medium-high heat in a pan.

Add salt, green chiles, pimento peppers, onions, cumin, chili powder, and these seasonings for 2 to 3 minutes. Add the cheese once the tomato paste has been combined. Get rid of the heat. Place a little amount of the beef mixture—about two tablespoons—in the middle of each pie crust circle. Seal the dough along the curved edge using a fork after folding it over. Place on the baking sheet prepared in a single layer, not touching. Apply egg wash to the empanadas—10 minutes in the oven or until golden brown. Traditional guacamole should be given some time to chill before serving. Enjoy!

Notes

Prepare ahead of time:
These freeze exceptionally well when kept in an airtight container. For a later, fast, and simple lunch, you may bake first and then freeze after. Reheat in the microwave individually or in groups of 2-3.

GUACAMOLE

Prep Time: 15 mins
Total Time: 15 mins

Ingredients

- Three avocados - peeled
- One lime, juiced
- One teaspoon of minced garlic
- 1 pinch ground cayenne pepper
- One teaspoon salt
- Two plum tomatoes
- ½ cup diced onion
- Three tablespoons chopped fresh cilantro

Directions

Add the mashed avocados, lime juice, salt, and cilantro to a medium bowl with tomatoes, onion, and garlic. Stir in the cayenne pepper. For more excellent flavor, cover and refrigerate for an hour before serving.

PINEAPPLE SAUCE

Prep Time: 10 mins
Cook Time: 10 mins
Total Time: 20 mins

Ingredients

- ¾ cup pineapple juice
- Two tablespoons of teriyaki sauce
- 1 ½ tablespoons garlic powder
- ¼ cup water
- One teaspoon of soy sauce
- ½ teaspoon lemon juice
- Four slices of canned pineapple in juice, drained and chopped

- ½ cup white sugar

Directions

Combine the pineapple juice, teriyaki sauce, lemon juice, soy sauce, pineapple, sugar, and garlic powder in a sizable saucepan over medium heat. The liquid has to cook for around 5 minutes before it turns into syrup. Cook the mixture while stirring in the water until it thickens once more. Serve right away after removing from heat.

CHICKEN LETTUCE WRAPS

Prep Time: 30 mins
Cook Time: 20 mins
Total Time: 50 mins

Ingredients

- 1 ½ pounds ground chicken
- One red bell pepper, cut into large dice
- One tablespoon chopped green onion
- One tablespoon of chopped fresh cilantro
- ½ cup soy sauce
- Two tablespoons rice wine vinegar, or more to taste
- One tablespoon of grated fresh ginger
- Five dashes of hot pepper sauce
- One teaspoon of sesame oil
- ½ cup chunky peanut butter
- Three tablespoons of hot water
- Three tablespoons soy sauce
- Five dashes of hot pepper sauce
- Six large leaves of iceberg lettuce
- Two carrots, shredded

Directions

For 10 minutes, stir ground chicken in a big pan until the flesh is crumbly and no longer pink. Remove extra grease.

Red bell pepper is added to the chicken, and the mixture is cooked and stirred for five more minutes.

Combine 1/2 cup soy sauce, five dashes spicy sauce, ginger, rice wine vinegar, and sesame oil in a bowl. Pour over the chicken mixture. Cook and toss the chicken mixture with the sauce over low heat for 5-10 mins to combine the flavors. Mix the peanut butter and hot water in a sizable bowl and mash until smooth. Add the soy sauce and hot pepper sauce and whisk to combine. Remove the dipping sauce.

Make cups out of lettuce leaves and fill them with the chicken mixture. Shredded carrots, green onion, cilantro, and a teaspoon of peanut dipping sauce go on top of lettuce wraps.

SHRIMP CHOWDER

Prep Time: 15 mins
Cook Time: 3 hrs 30mins
Total Time: 3 hrs 45mins
Servings:12

Ingredients

- ½ cup chopped onion
- Two teaspoons butter
- One teaspoon of Creole seasoning
- Two ib peeled and deveined cooked small shrimp
- ½ teaspoon garlic powder
- 3 ounces cream cheese
- Two cans (12 ounces each) of evaporated milk
- Two cans (10-3/4 ounces each) of condensed cream of potato soup
- Two cans (10-3/4 ounces each) of condensed cream of chicken soup
- One can (7 ounces) of white corn

Directions

Cook onion in butter in a small pan until it turns soft. Combine the onion, milk, soups, corn, creole spice, and garlic powder in a 5-qt. Slow cooker.3 hours on low heat with a cover. Cream cheese and shrimp are combined. Cook for 30 mins until the cheese is melted and the shrimp well-cooked. To mix, stir.

PERUVIAN SCALLOP

Prep Time: 10 mins
Cook Time: 10 mins
Optional saltwater soak:30mins
Total Time: 50 mins
Servings: 4

Ingredients

- 12 large sea scallops, about a pound
- Ice
- One lemon juiced
- Two tablespoons of sea salt
- One quarter water
- Avocado Yogurt Sauce
- One medium avocado skin and pit removed
- 1/2 cup plain nonfat Greek yogurt
- One shallot minced
- One clove of garlic minced
- Two teaspoons ají amarillo paste
- 1/3 cup passionfruit juice
- One lime juiced
- ½ cup cilantro packed
- ½ teaspoon sea salt
- Fresh ground pepper
- Water, buttermilk, milk to thin
- Passionfruit Ají Amarillo Sauce

- Four tablespoons butter
- One tablespoon of fresh lime juice
- 1/2 teaspoon sea salt

Directions

If you're using "wet" scallops, wash them for 30 minutes in an arrangement that includes 1 quart of cold water,1/4 cup of lemon juice, a few ice cubes, and two teaspoons of table salt.

Over medium heat, include butter, shallot, and garlic to a sauté pan. for two to three minutes. Add the aj amarillo paste and dijon mustard. To blend, stir. Include another 2 to 3 mins of cooking.

Stir in the passionfruit purée after adding it. Add the fresh lime juice after turning the heat off. Scrape ingredients into a little food processor, then process until smooth. If necessary, taste and add sea salt and freshly ground pepper. Place aside.

Fill a food processor with the ingredients for the avocado sauce. Once smooth, verify and taste-test the seasoning before continuing. To make it thick yet pourable, thin with a bit of water.
Toss the scallops with sea salt and freshly ground pepper after patting them dry.

Put a thin layer of oil on the pan and heat it. Put the scallops that you've prepared on the heated surface. Turn them after 1.5 to 2 minutes. They should be relatively simple to flip if they are ready. Heat to a medium setting. Cook for a further 1.5 to 2 minutes. Get rid of the heat.

Notes

Add a touch of your preferred liquid sweetener if the sauce is too tart for your taste. The avocado sauce and the scallops balance out the tartness that we prefer.

RED SALAD

Prep Time: 15 mins
Additional Time: 8 hrs
Total Time: 8 hrs 15 mins

Ingredients

- ⅔ cup red wine vinegar
- ½ cup canola oil
- ¼ teaspoon ground black pepper
- ¼ teaspoon onion powder
- One head of red cabbage, cored and shredded
- One tablespoon of white sugar
- One teaspoon salt
- One teaspoon of seasoned salt

Directions

In a bowl, combine the following ingredients: red wine vinegar, canola oil, sugar, salt, seasoned salt, pepper, and onion powder.
In a large glass dish, place the cabbage. Toss the cabbage with the dressing to coat. Cover and chill for 10-12 hrs, stirring periodically. Before serving, drain.

TAMALITOS VERDES

Prep Time:45 mins
Total Time: 1hr 15 mins
Servings:12

Ingredients

For the sauce:

- One red onion
- 1 Peruvian yellow pepper
- Fresh cilantro
- Salt and pepper
- Juice of 1 lemon

For the tamales:

- 2 lb fresh corn, loose kernels
- 2 cups cilantro leaves
- Salt and pepper
- Three tablespoons sugar
- 1 cup oil
- Fresh corn husks
- 1 cup fresh spinach
- ½ cup vegetable oil
- ½ cup chopped onion
- ½ cup Peruvian yellow pepper
- Three garlic cloves, chopped

Directions

Julienne cut the red onion into thin strips for the sauce, then rinsed them in cool water. Drain and combine with salt, pepper, lemon juice, cilantro leaves, and Peruvian yellow pepper that has been roughly julienned. Olive oil is added at the very last step.

For the tamales, combine the maize, cilantro, and spinach. Remember that too much moisture in the maize can ruin the tamales' texture. Place the corn that has been processed in the container. Heat the oil in a sizable frying pan on medium heat. When the onion is ready but not overdone, add it and cook it while stirring. Add the garlic and processed yellow pepper and cook for a few more minutes. Before adding anything to the processed corn, combine everything. Use a wooden spoon to stir the meal for approximately 15 minutes while seasoning it with salt, pepper, and sugar.

While you wait, remove the corn husks. To build the tamales, stack two corn husks on each other and place two tablespoons of the dough in the middle. Fold the cornhusks into the shape of the tamales, and then cut a strip from each one that will be knotted in the middle.

A layer of cornhusks must be laid at a large pot's bottom. There, place the tamales. Add 3 cups of water, more corn husks, a lid, and a boil. The tamales will cook for around 25 minutes. Cut the heat and let it cool.

If you want to eat the tamales immediately, allowing them to cool is crucial so they fail to crumble when you open them.
Give each person a serving of criolla salsa and two tamales.

HUANCAYO-STYLE POTATOES

Prep Time: 20 mins
Cook Time: 25 mins
Total Time: 45 mins

Ingredients

- 12 Yukon Gold potatoes
- One tablespoon olive oil, or to taste
- Eight leaves lettuce
- Four large hard-boiled eggs
- Eight black olives
- One onion, sliced

- Six chile peppers, halved lengthwise and seeded
- 1 pound cream cheese, softened
- 1 pound queso fresco, crumbled
- ¼ cup vegetable oil
- Two teaspoons salt
- One clove garlic
- ½ teaspoon ground black pepper
- ⅓ cup evaporated milk

Directions

To boil:
1. Add salted water to a large saucepan with the potatoes.
2. Once the meat is cooked, simmer for about 20 minutes before lowering the heat to medium.
3. Drain, then allow to cool gradually.

Olive oil must be heated in a pan over medium heat. Cook and sauté the onion for about 10 minutes in the hot oil. Remove the heat.

A small pan of water has been heated to a rolling boil. The required boiling time for softening chili peppers is five minutes. To make the chiles feasible, run them under cold water before removing and discarding the skins.

The mixture should be smooth after being well blended with the onion, chile peppers, cream cheese, queso fresco, oil, salt, and pepper. While the blender is running, gently add evaporated milk to the combined liquid as the sauce thickens.

Each of the six dishes should have one lettuce leaf on it. After halving the potatoes, arrange three halves on each lettuce leaf— sauce over the potatoes. Two olive halves and half of an egg should be placed on each plate.

PERUVIAN SAUSAGES AND POTATOES

Prep Time:15 minutes
Cook Time:15 minutes
Total Time:30 minutes
Servings:2 -4

Ingredients

- Vegetable oil for frying
- Two russet potatoes
- Four beef hot dogs or sausages
- For Serving:
- Freshly chopped parsley
- Mayonnaise
- Ketchup
- Mustard
- Aji Amarillo Paste

Directions

Over medium-high heat, add at least 2 inches of vegetable oil to a deep saucepan. Paper towels must be used to cover a large piece of food altogether.

Potatoes must be peeled and sliced into fries between 1/3 and 1/2 inch broad. Add the potatoes in batches after the oil reaches a temperature of around 350 °F. Fry till golden and then move to the plate covered with towels.

Over medium heat, add roughly one teaspoon of oil to a big pan. Add the oval-shaped hot dogs to the preheated pan after thinly slicing them. Cook, periodically stirring, until fully cooked and browned. Toss in the fried potatoes after adding them.
For dipping, serve hot with mayonnaise, mustard, aji amarillo, parsley, and ketchup.

PERUVIAN AJI SAUCE

Prep Time: 10 mins
Total Time: 10 minutes
Servings: 1

Ingredients

- 2 cups lightly packed fresh cilantro
- ½ cup mayonnaise
- Two medium jalapeños, chopped
- Two cloves garlic, chopped
- 1/3 cup grated Cotija
- One tablespoon of lime juice
- 1/4 teaspoon fine sea salt

Directions

All of the ingredients must be combined in a food processor or blender. Blend the sauce until it is mainly smooth, and the cilantro is broken into small pieces. Taste, and if required, adjust. This sauce, which is intentionally robust and spicy, is great as written.

However, if the flavor is overpowering, add one tbsp of olive oil while the food processor runs.

Add some saved jalapeno seeds and remix them if it requires more heat.Add another tablespoon of lime juice and a dash of salt if it lacks flavor. For approximately a week, aji verde remains nicely in the refrigerator, covered.

Notes

Leave out the Parmesan. While the food processor works, add one to two teaspoons of olive oil to soften the taste.

You could skip the cheese and use equal portions of vegan sour cream for the mayonnaise. Try my avocado dip for a similarly creamy cilantro sauce. If you like it to be spicier, add additional jalapenos.

PERUVIAN MINESTRONE SOUP

Prep Time: 20 mins
Cook Time: 20 mins
Total Time: 40 mins
Servings: 4

Ingredients

- 6 cups of flavorful beef broth or bone broth
- 2 cups water
- 4 oz queso fresco cheese- diced into small 1/2 inch cubes - divided
- 4 oz Penne Rigata
- 1 –2 tablespoons olive oil
- salt and pepper
- Two fat shallots, diced
- Four garlic cloves, chopped
- 1/2 cup corn kernels
- 1/2 cup peas
- 1/2 cup carrots
- Two Yukon gold potatoes
- 8 ounces fresh baby spinach leaves
- 1 lb beef flank steak slice into small 3/4 inch cubes
- 8 oz fresh basil leaves

Directions

Heat water and beef stock over high heat in a big saucepan until it boils. Simultaneously, cook shallot and garlic until aromatic and brown in a large pan with olive oil over medium heat. Reduce the heat, then whisk in the spinach until it wilts. Stir in the basil until it has wilted.

Blend the spinach/basil combination with one-third of the queso fresco cheese, one to two cups of the stock/water mixture, and other ingredients. Until extremely smooth, blend. Place aside.

Add meat after the liquid has come to a boil. Peas, carrots, potatoes, and corn are added after bringing to a simmer. Add the pasta after 5 minutes of simmering. Cook for 8 mins or until al dente. Turn off the stove. Stir after adding the spinach mixture.

Serve the soup with the remaining cheese.

PERUVIAN PICKLED ONIONS

Prep Time: 30 mins
Additional Time: 40 mins
Total Time: 1 hrs 10 mins

Ingredients

- One teaspoon of sea salt
- Two red onions
- 1 ½ teaspoons olive oil
- cracked black pepper
- Two large English cucumbers
- One large tomato
- Two tablespoons of rice vinegar
- Two tablespoons of lime juice
- One tablespoon of white wine vinegar
- One jalapeno pepper
- One tablespoon of chopped fresh cilantro

Directions

Salt should be dissolved in water once it has been added. Red onions can be added; soak for 10 minutes. Drain and pat oneself dry.

Combine onions, cucumbers, tomatoes, rice vinegar, lime juice, white wine vinegar, olive oil, jalapeño pepper, cilantro, and black pepper in a large bowl. Before serving, let the food marinate at room temperature for about 30 minutes under plastic wrap.

PERUVIAN POTATOES

Prep Time: 15 mins
Cook Time: 45 mins
Total Time: 1 hr
Servings: 4 to 6

Ingredients

- 2 pounds Peruvian purple potatoes
- ½ cup extra-virgin olive oil
- Salt and freshly ground black pepper
- One tablespoon cilantro
- One tablespoon of Mexican oregano
- One tablespoon of minced garlic

Directions

Set oven to 400 degrees Fahrenheit. The potatoes must be cut in half and put in a basin. If you chop them ahead of time, cover them with water.

In a separate bowl, combine olive oil, oregano, garlic, salt, and pepper. Mix thoroughly. Add potatoes to the oil mixture after simply draining them. Combine the olive oil and toss. On a sheet pan, spread the potatoes out. Potatoes should be soft after 30 minutes of grilling. Add cilantro and then serve.

CEVICHE PERUANO

Prep Time: 30 mins
Cook Time: 40 mins
Additional Time: 1 hrs
Total Time: 2 hrs 10 mins

Ingredients

- Two potatoes
- Two sweet potatoes
- 1 pound medium shrimp - peeled, deveined
- One bibb or Boston lettuce
- One red onion, cut into thin strips
- 1 cup fresh lime juice
- ½ stalk celery
- ¼ cup lightly packed cilantro leaves
- 1 pinch ground cumin
- One clove of garlic, minced
- One habanero pepper
- Salt and freshly ground pepper to taste
- 1 pound fresh tilapia

Directions

Add water to a saucepan with the potatoes and sweet potatoes. Drain and let the potatoes cool to average temperature after simmering until they can be readily pierced with a fork. After soaking the onion slices in warm water for ten minutes, rinse them and set them aside.

In the meantime, combine the lime juice, celery, cilantro, and cumin in a blender and process until completely smooth. Put the habanero pepper and garlic into a large glass bowl with the mixture. Add the diced tilapia and shrimp after seasoning with salt and pepper.

Stirring periodically, set aside for an hour to marinate. The seafood is complete once it turns firm and opaque.

Peel the potatoes and slice them before serving. Add the onions to the combination of fish. With lettuce leaves, line-filling meals. Place the ceviche in the dishes with its juice and add potato slices as a garnish.

ROTISSERIE CHICKEN, WITH FRIED YUCCA ROOT

Prep Time: 30 min
Inactive Time: 2 hr
Cook Time: 1 hr 55 min
Total Time: 4 hr 25 min
Servings : 4

Ingredients:

- One whole chicken
- One teaspoon of minced garlic
- Three lemons or limes juiced
- ½ teaspoon annatto
- 2 pounds yucca root
- Vegetable oil for frying
- Two tablespoons of Peruvian herb
- One teaspoon pepper
- One teaspoon salt
- 2 Peruvian chile
- ½ teaspoon ground cumin

Aji sauce:
- 1 cup of cream of aji (6 -8 ajies in the blender with salt, one clove of garlic, ground
- black pepper, and ½ cup oil)
- 1 ½ tablespoons olive oil
- Two green onions, chopped
- Two tablespoons of lime juice

Creamy cheese sauce:
- One package of queso fresco
- ¼ red onion sauteed
- Salt and freshly ground black pepper
- One tablespoon of lemon juice
- ¾ cup oil
- ¾ cup milk
- One teaspoon turmeric
- One aji chile

Directions

Rotisserie chicken must be thoroughly rinsed, and all fat must be removed. The chicken's wings must be tucked beneath its back. Combine the garlic, huacatay, pepper, salt, aji, cumin, lemon or lime juice, and achiote to create a paste. Apply the paste to the chicken and thoroughly massage it outside. For an excellent taste, let it remain in the refrigerator for at least two hours. Set oven to 350 degrees Fahrenheit. In the roasting pan with a cover, place the chicken. Cook for 1 1/2 hrs with the lid on or until golden brown.

Yucca Root:

Following the yucca's peeling and boiling. It must be shaped like a French fry. Heat the oil to 340-360 degrees Fahrenheit in a deep pot or deep fryer. If necessary, fry the yucca in batches until crispy and golden. Salt to taste, if desired.

Aji sauce:
In a medium bowl, combine the cream of aji, green onions, olive oil, and lime juice.

Cheese sauce:
In a blender, combine queso fresco, red onion, oil, milk, turmeric combination, chile, salt, pepper, and lemon juice until well combined. Place the chicken on a platter, surrounded by the fried yucca root, with the two sauces on the side for dipping.

FRIED STUFFED POTATOE

Prep Time: 1 hrs
Cook Time: 45 mins
Additional Time: 2 hrs 30 mins
Total Time: 4 hrs 15 mins

Ingredients

- Four large potatoes, peeled and cubed
- 1 ½ teaspoons salt, divided
- 2 cups dry bread crumbs
- 1 cup all-purpose flour
- One tablespoon of vegetable oil
- One green bell pepper, chopped
- ½ cup chopped onion
- Three cloves garlic, minced
- 1 pound ground beef
- Four teaspoons of tomato paste
- One tablespoon of distilled white vinegar
- Two teaspoons of ground cumin
- One teaspoon of ground black pepper
- Four large eggs
- One-quarter of vegetable oil for frying

Directions

Put the potatoes in a big saucepan and add the salted water. Heat to a boil over high heat, then lower to a simmer, cover, and cook for 20 minutes or until the vegetables are softened. Drain and let steam dry for a minute or two.

Mash potatoes with 1/2 teaspoon salt in a bowl until no lumps are visible. After cooling to room temperature, set aside.

Meanwhile, warm up some vegetable oil in a large pan over medium heat. In a heated skillet, stir green pepper, onion, and garlic for approximately 10 minutes or until the onion is soft and translucent.

Turn the heat up to medium-high and add the ground meat. Cook and stir the meat until it is pink no more and crumbly. Once the tomato paste has dissolved, add the vinegar, cumin, one teaspoon salt, and pepper. Place the beef mixture in a bowl and let it cool to room temperature.

Wax paper or plastic wrap must line a baking sheet; keep it aside. Beat eggs in a mixing bowl; place aside. Put flour and bread crumbs in separate, shallow plates and leave aside.

Divide a handful of mashed potatoes (about 1/12 of the total) into two equal servings. Fill each piece with the beef mixture after forming it into a tiny bowl shape. To form a ball, place the pieces together, seal the edges, and smooth. Repeat this step with the rest of the potatoes and beef mixture.

Gently coat each potato ball in flour, one at a time; brush off the extra. Roll in bread crumbs after dipping in beaten egg. To ensure that all bread crumbs fall off, gently toss them in your hands. Put the breaded potato balls on the baking sheet that has been prepared. Either freeze for later use or refrigerate for two to four hours.

The desired temperature is 350° F (175° C) of oil in a deep fryer or big saucepan.

Cook potato balls until crispy and golden brown in heated oil in batches, about 3 minutes for each set, rolling the balls around as they cook for even frying.

ROCOTO RELLENO

Prep Time: 20 mins
Cook Time: 1 hrs 40 mins
Total Time: 2 hrs

Ingredients

- 4 cups water
- 2 cups brown rice
- Six red bell peppers, tops, and seeds removed
- ¼ cup grated Parmesan cheese, or to taste
- 1 pound ground beef
- One onion, diced
- ¼ cup chopped mushrooms
- Three cloves garlic, chopped
- 26-ounce tomato sauce
- 16-ounce diced tomatoes
- 6-ounce tomato paste
- One teaspoon of Italian seasoning
- salt and ground black pepper to taste

Directions

In a pan, brown rice and water are brought to a boil. Lessen the heat to medium-low, cover, and simmer up to rice is tender and liquid has been absorbed, about 40 minutes; transfer cooked rice into a large mixing bowl.

350°F/175°C) should be the preheated oven temperature. In the meantime, preheat a big skillet over medium-high heat. After breaking it into small pieces, please put the ground beef in the skillet. When the meat is thoroughly browned, include the mushrooms, onion, and garlic. Cook and stir for 7 to 10 mins—the meat mixture with brown rice. Season the rice mixture with salt & pepper after adding the tomato sauce, chopped tomatoes, tomato paste, and Italian seasoning.

On a baking sheet, arrange the bell peppers and fill them thoroughly with the mixture. The peppers should be baked in the oven for about an hour or until tender. Add Parmesan cheese to the stuffed peppers before serving.

PERUVIAN BEANS AND RICE

Prep Time: 15 mins
Cook Time: 15mins
Total Time: 30 mins
Servings: 2

Ingredients

- One small red onion
- Two tablespoons chopped fresh cilantro
- 2 cups cooked or canned canary beans
- 1 cup cold cooked white rice
- One tablespoon chopped flat-leaf parsley
- One tablespoon chopped fresh oregano
- One lime
- Two tablespoons of fresh lime juice
- ¼ teaspoon kosher salt
- Three teaspoons of hot pepper sauce
- Three tablespoons grape-seed oil
- Two garlic cloves, chopped
- ½ teaspoon kosher salt

Directions

To make criolla salsa:
1. Cover the sliced onion with cold water.
2. Drain after 10 minutes of sitting.
3. Combine cilantro, lime juice, 1/4 teaspoon kosher salt, and two tablespoons of hot sauce with the onion slices before serving.

Into a 10-inch nonstick pan, add one tablespoon of vegetable or grape-seed oil and heat it over medium-high heat. Add the chopped onion and garlic, and stir—Sauté for 5 to 6 minutes or until aromatic. Scrape into a food processor bowl and add 1/2 teaspoon kosher salt and one tsp hot pepper sauce paste. Wipe the skillet.

One cup of beans should be added to a food processor and briefly pureed until smooth but still lumpy. Put into ample food. Add the rice, parsley, and oregano with 1 cup of beans, according to taste.
Pour one tablespoon of grape-seed oil into the same skillet and heat it to medium. Once the oil is shimmering, add the bean mixture and lightly compress it with a spatula. Cook for 7 minutes or until the bottom is well-browned.

Take the skillet from the heat, place a dish on top, and carefully flip the bean mixture so the browned side faces up. Slide the bean mixture back into the skillet, reheat to medium, and add one tablespoon of grape-seed oil. Seven more minutes of cooking or until browned. Remove from heat and turn the plate over the skillet. Serve hot with lime wedges and criolla salsa on the side.

QUESO FRESCO

Prep Time: 4 mins
Cook Time: 15 mins
Rest and Chill: 4 hrs
Total:4 hrs 19 mins
Servings: 16

Ingredients

- 1-gallon whole milk
- One teaspoon of kosher salt
- One teaspoon of liquid rennet

Direction

Gather the ingredients. Whole milk should be gradually heated in a big saucepan over low heat until it reaches 100 F (38 C). Stir in the liquid rennet after taking the milk off the heat.

Until the milk hardens into a custardy mass, leave the mixture in an area of warmth for 1 to 2 hours. The ideal way to maintain the temperature during this period is to either place the pot in an oven with the viewing or pilot light on but the oven off or to immerse the bottom half of the pot in warm water in a sink.

Break the mixture once the curds have developed until they are the size of peas. If you'd like, use a knife, although it's better to use clean hands. The whey should drain from the curd for 20 to 30 minutes after being poured into a colander with 2 to 4 cheesecloths.

Add one teaspoon of salt to the drained curds using clean hands or a spoon in the mixing bowl. Avoid overmixing the cheese since it could lose its ideal crumbly texture and become creamier.

Put the salted curds into a cheesecloth, buttered muslin-lined cheese mold, or a colander set in a large bowl or the sink.

Wrap the cheese ball securely in the cloth. Drain it for approximately an hour or until it becomes reasonably firm. The queso fresco should be unwrapped and chilled for an hour before usage.

How to Store Queso Fresco

Queso fresco should be kept chilled in covered food storage containers. When producing the cheese, remember that it should be consumed within a week. Put it, completely covered, in the refrigerator's coldest section.

BUTTERNUT SQUASH

Prep Time: 15 mins
Cook Time: 25 mins
Total Time: 40 mins

Ingredients

- One medium butternut squash
- Two tablespoons of olive oil
- Two cloves garlic
- salt and ground black pepper to taste

Directions

Heat the oven to 200 degrees C.Use a sharp vegetable peeler to keep away the butternut squash skin. Scoop out and discard seeds after cutting in half lengthwise. Make 1-inch slices from the halves, then 1-inch cubes from the pieces.

Combine butternut squash cubes, olive oil, and garlic; toss to coat evenly. Add salt and pepper to taste. Put on a baking sheet in a single layer.

Roast in the oven for 33-35 mins or until the squash is slightly browned and easily punctured with a fork.

ARROZ TAPADO

Prep Time: 20 mins
Cook Time: 55 mins
Additional Time: 15 mins
Total Time: 1 hrs 30 mins

Ingredients

- 2 cups uncooked white rice
- 4 cups water
- One teaspoon of chopped fresh tomato
- One teaspoon ketchup
- One egg
- One potato, peeled and cubed
- 1 cup vegetable oil for frying
- Three small tomatoes, coarsely chopped
- ½ cup water
- One tablespoon of vegetable oil
- ½ large onion, finely chopped
- Three cloves garlic, chopped
- One teaspoon ground dried aji chile
- ½ teaspoon ground cumin
- ¼ teaspoon ground black pepper
- Two teaspoons of chopped fresh oregano
- 1 pound lean ground beef
- Two large carrots, peeled and cubed
- ¼ cup frozen peas
- One tablespoon of peanut butter
- One teaspoon of chopped fresh cilantro

Directions

Carry the rice and 4 cups of water to a boil in a saucepan over high heat. Lessen the heat to medium-low, cover the pot, and simmer for 22-25 mins, or until the rice is totally cooked and the liquid is fully absorbed.

Put the egg in a saucepan and add enough water to cover it by one inch. Water should be brought to a boil over high heat with the lid on the pan. The egg should be left in boiling water for 15 minutes after the heat source has been turned off. After draining the hot water, chill the egg in the sink's running cold water. Once cooled, peel. The egg should be chopped and placed in a small basin.

Heat 1 cup of vegetable oil to 350 degrees F (175 degrees C) in a deep fryer or big saucepan. The potato cubes should be deep-fried for about 5 mins or until golden brown; drain on paper towels, and leave aside.

Blend tomatoes with 1/2 cup of water until they are entirely smooth. Heat one tablespoon of vegetable oil on medium heat in a large pan. Cook and stir the onion, garlic, aji chile powder, cumin, black pepper, and oregano for 8 to 10 minutes or until the onion starts to brown. Then, add the pureed tomatoes and simmer for five more minutes, stirring often. Add the ground beef and carrots, and simmer for 10 minutes until the meat is no longer pink and the vegetables are soft. As the meat cooks cut it into little pieces. Until well blended, stir in the chopped hard-boiled egg, peas, and peanut butter. The fried potato cubes are then carefully incorporated.

Oil a flexible plastic bowl (at least 1 cup) for the dish's assembly, then push cooked rice into the bottom to fill up about one-third. Then, add enough cooked rice to fill the bowl on top of the meat mixture to cover the rice by approximately 3/4 inch. Place a serving dish on top of the bowl, flip it over, and turn out the rice and meat-filled form after gently pressing it with an oiled palm to compact the mixture. Add the remaining ingredients and repeat. On each plate, garnish with sprinklings of cilantro, chunks of tomato, and dollops of ketchup.

PERUVIAN GREEN BEANS WITH CHICKEN

Prep Time: 15 mins
Cook Time: 25 mins
Total Time: 40 mins

Ingredients

- One tablespoon of canola oil divided
- Three cloves garlic, minced
- Three tablespoons white wine vinegar
- salt to taste
- 1 cup chopped cilantro
- Two chile peppers,
- One ¼ pound of chicken cut into 1-inch cubes
- Six tablespoons soy sauce divided
- One tablespoon of ground cumin divided
- One red onion, halved and sliced
- Four plum tomatoes, cut into eighths
- 12-ounce packages of frozen French-style green beans

Directions

Heat half the canola oil over medium-high heat in a wok or big skillet. In heated oil, cook garlic and chile peppers for approximately a minute or until aromatic. To the wok, add the chicken. Cook the chicken combination for 5 to 7 minutes, or just until the chicken is no longer pink in the center, after stirring in half the soy sauce and half the cumin. Reheat the mixture after transferring it to a bowl while keeping some drippings in the skillet.

In the skillet with the saved drippings, heat the remaining oil. Cook and toss the onion in the oil mixture for about 5 minutes, adding the remaining soy sauce and cumin. Include the tomatoes in the onion mixture, and simmer and stir for approximately a minute or until the tomatoes soften.Add the chicken mixture to the pan, vinegar, and green beans. For 10 minutes, stir the mixture until the green beans are cooked. Add salt and cilantro to the mix and toss to combine.

PERUVIAN CILANTRO RICE

Prep Time: 15 mins
Cook Time: 20 mins
Total Time: 35 mins

Ingredients

- 2 (4 ounces) skinless, boneless chicken breast halves
- One bunch of fresh cilantro,
- ½ cup water
- One tablespoon of vegetable oil
- One tablespoon of minced garlic
- ¼ cup frozen chopped carrots
- ¼ cup frozen peas
- salt and freshly ground black pepper
- One tablespoon cumin
- 1 cup uncooked white rice

Directions

Add the chicken to a big pot, and then add about 3 cups of water to cover. After bringing it to a boil, cook for about fifteen minutes or up to the chicken is cooked. Chicken must be diced, with cooking liquid saved.

Cilantro and 1/2 cup water must be pureed in a food processor or blender.Garlic is cooked in hot oil until just beginning to brown. 2 cups of the cooking liquid must be added, followed by the rice, cilantro puree, chopped chicken, carrots, peas, and cumin. To taste, include salt and pepper in the food. Carry to a simmer, cover, and cook on low heat for 15 to 20 minutes or until the rice is cooked and the liquid has been absorbed.

PERUVIAN ALFAJORES WITH MANJAR BLANCO

Prep Time: 1 hrs
Cook Time: 40 mins
Additional Time: 30 mins
Total Time: 2 hrs 10 mins

Ingredients

- 2 cups white sugar
- Three sticks butter
- Two teaspoons of vanilla extract
- One teaspoon of baking powder
- Three tablespoons water, or as needed
- Two tablespoons confectioners' sugar, or as needed
- 5 cups cornstarch
- 2 cups all-purpose flour
- Four eggs
- Three tablespoons pisco

Manjar Blanco:
- 14-ounce cans of sweetened condensed milk
- 6-ounce evaporated milk
- ¼ cup brown sugar
- ¼ cup confectioners' sugar, or to taste

Directions

Set the oven's temperature to 300 °F (150 °C). Combine white sugar and butter in a large bowl using an electric mixer and beat up to smooth. Add the baking powder, pisco, vanilla extract, cornstarch, flour, and eggs. Gently blend by combining.

On a clean work area, spread the dough and knead it by hand until it is smooth. As necessary, add water. Cut in half, put one half in the fridge, and leave the other out.

Sprinkle powdered sugar all over your work surface. With a cookie cutter or shot glass, cut the dough into 2-inch circles after rolling it out to a 1/4-inch thickness. On a baking sheet, arrange the rounds closely together. With a fork, prick each biscuit twice.

The cookies should still be white and soft, not crunchy, after 10 minutes of baking in the preheated oven. The cookies will become more solid as they continue to cool. Use the leftover cookie dough to repeat.

Brown sugar, evaporated milk, and condensed milk should all be combined in a pot over low heat. Continually stir the filling for 20 to 30 minutes until it approaches thick caramel consistency. Remove from heat; mixture will begin to firm up after 30 minutes at room temperature.

Confectioners' sugar must be put into a small basin. Over the cooled cookies, spread roughly 1/2 tbsp of the filling. To create the alfajores, combine every pair of cookies. Sprinkle confectioners' sugar over alfajores.

TARTAR SAUCE

Prep Time: 15 mins
Additional Time: 2 hrs
Total Time: 2 hrs 15 mins
Servings: 1

Ingredients

- 1 cup mayonnaise
- Two tablespoons chopped onion
- One dash of hot pepper sauce
- One dash of Worcestershire sauce
- Two tablespoons chopped dill pickles

- Two tablespoons chopped sweet pickles
- One tablespoon of chopped fresh parsley
- One tablespoon of fresh lemon juice
- One teaspoon of chopped capers
- One teaspoon of prepared yellow mustard

Directions

Mayonnaise, onion, sweet and dill pickles, parsley, lemon juice, capers, mustard, spicy sauce, and Worcestershire sauce should all be assembled in a bowl. Chill in the fridge for at least two hours to melt the flavors.

HOGAO RECIPE

Prep Time: 5 mins
Cook Time: 15 mins
Total Time: 20 mins
Servings: 2

Ingredients

- Three tablespoons vegetable oil
- 1 cup chopped scallions
- 2 cups diced tomato
- One clove of garlic minced
- One teaspoon of ground cumin
- ¼ teaspoon salt
- ¼ teaspoon ground pepper

Directions

The tomatoes, scallions, garlic, and ground cumin are added to the hot oil in the pan and gently cook for 10 minutes while stirring to soften the ingredients. Include the salt, turn the heat low, and simmer for 10 mins, stirring now and again, until the sauce has thickened. Check and adjust the seasoning.

Notes

Keep in the refrigerator for up to a week in a sealed container.

PICO DE GALLO

Prep Time: 20 mins
Total Time: 20 mins

Ingredients

- Six plum tomatoes
- ½ red onion, minced
- 1 pinch ground cumin
- salt and ground black pepper to taste
- Three tablespoons chopped fresh cilantro
- ½ jalapeño pepper, seeded and minced
- ½ lime, juiced
- One clove of garlic, minced
- One pinch of garlic powder

Directions

Gather all ingredients.Combine the tomatoes, onion, cilantro, jalapenos, lime juice, garlic, garlic powder, cumin, salt, and pepper in a bowl.

AJÍ PICANTE

Prep Time: 20 mins
Servings: 2

Ingredients

- 1 seeded small hot pepper
- ½ cup white vinegar
- ½ cup chopped scallions
- ½ cup chopped tomato
- ¼ cup water
- ¼ teaspoon salt

- One teaspoon sugar
- One tablespoon of lime juice
- Two tablespoons of vegetable oil
- ½ cup chopped fresh cilantro
- ¼ cup chopped fresh parsley

Directions

For two minutes, mix the vinegar and habanero pepper in a blender. In a bowl, combine the remaining ingredients by stirring. Mix thoroughly after adding the vinegar and habanero mixture to the basin.Cover after pouring into a glass jar. Keep in the fridge for ten days.

Notes

A sealed container or jar of aji picante can be kept in the refrigerator for ten days.

AJÍ DE TOMATE DE ÁRBOL.

Prep Time:5 minutes
Cook Time:5 minutes
Total Time:10 minutes
Servings: 1

Ingredients

- 4-5 tree tomatoes fresh
- Two ajies
- Salt to taste
- Two tbs chopped white onion
- One tbs chopped cilantro
- One tbs lemon juice
- ¼ cup water

Directions

If using fresh tree tomatoes, boil them for around 5 minutes to simplify peeling.Split them in half when using frozen tree tomatoes and scoop out the insides after allowing them to thaw overnight in the refrigerator.

Combine the spicy peppers and tree tomatoes in a blender. Add the water to the small saucepan with the blended tree tomatoes and spicy peppers, and simmer for 5-8 minutes over medium heat. The sauce will be fresher if you skip the cooking step, but you'll need to eat it more quickly.

Add the chopped onion, cilantro, lime juice, chochos, and salt to taste—cold or warm serving.

Notes

For a creamier Cuencano-style aji, replace the water with light olive oil or a mildly flavored oil.

AJI HUACATAY

Prep Time:15 minutes
Total Time:15 minutes
Servings:4

Ingredients

For the huacatay sauce:
- Two cloves garlic chopped
- 2 Tablespoons Vegetable oil
- Salt and pepper to taste
- Three scallions roughly chopped
- 2 Tablespoons aji amarillo paste
- 2 Tablespoons huacatay paste
- 1/2 cup mayonnaise
- 3 Tablespoons chopped cilantro

Directions

Sauté in a small skillet filled with heated oil. the garlic on low heat

Garlic oil, scallions, mayonnaise, aji amarillo, huacatay, and cilantro should all be added to a blender and blended until smooth. When ready to use, season with salt and pepper and place in the refrigerator.

ABORRAJADOS DE PLÁTANO OR RIPE PLANTAIN FRITTERS.

Prep Time: 15 mins
Cook Time: 5 mins
Total Time: 20 mins
Servings: 8

Ingredients

- Two large, very ripe plantains
- Vegetable oil for frying
- Eight mozzarella cheese slices
- For the batter:
- Two eggs
- Four tablespoons flour
- Pinch salt

Directions

Cut the plantains crosswise into 8, 1 12" slices after peeling. Vegetable oil must be poured into a big saucepan and heated to 360 degrees. Plantain pieces should be added to the heated oil and fried for 3 minutes or until golden.

Make the batter by combining the salt, sugar, and flour in a small bowl. Eggs are added. Stir in the milk gradually to create a smooth batter. Place aside and wrap with plastic.
With a slotted spoon, remove the plantains and drain them on paper towels. On parchment paper or plastic, spread the plantain chunks out to a thickness of 14".

Make a sandwich by placing one plantain pattie with a cheese slice in the center, covering it with another pattie, then pressing the sides together to contain the cheese thoroughly.

Sandwiches are added to the oil in batches after having been coated in the batter. Fry up to golden brown and crisp, about a minute on each side. Use a slotted spoon to delete and drain on paper towels.

Notes

For this dish, use extremely ripe plantains.

ROASTED VEGGIE QUESADILLAS

Prep Time: 15 min.
Cook Time: 20 min.
Servings: 12

Ingredients

- One medium onion, chopped
- One medium zucchini, chopped
- Guacamole
- sour cream
- salsa and sliced ripe olives
- One medium sweet red pepper, chopped
- 1 cup frozen corn, thawed
- One tablespoon of olive oil
- ½ teaspoon ground cumin
- Four tomato flour tortillas
- 1 cup shredded Mexican cheese blend

Directions

The oven to 425 degrees. The vegetables, oil, and cumin should all be combined in a big basin and covered. Place in a 15x10x1-inch baking pan that has not been oiled in a single layer. Bake uncovered for 10-15 minutes or until tender. Heat to 350 degrees.

Between two tortillas, evenly spread the vegetable mixture. Grate some cheese on top.Add the remaining tortillas on top. Put on an ungreased baking sheet and bake for 8-10 mins or until the cheese melts. Each quesadilla is divided into six wedges.Olives, salsa, sour cream, and guacamole are optional garnishes.

PERUVIAN PORK

Prep Time: 1 hrs
Cook Time: 40 mins
Total Time: 1 hrs 40 mins

Ingredients

- 2 ½ pounds of boneless pork shoulder, cubed
- ¼ cup white vinegar
- One tablespoon of all-purpose flour
- Two tablespoons water
- One tablespoon of ground cumin
- One tablespoon of ground turmeric
- ½ teaspoon garlic powder
- One teaspoon salt, or to taste
- ¼ teaspoon ground black pepper, or to taste
- One tablespoon of vegetable oil
- 1 cup orange juice
- ½ cup water
- One tablespoon of dried minced onion

Directions

Put the meat in a large basin. In a small bowl, combine the vinegar, cumin, turmeric, garlic powder, salt, and pepper. Stir to coat the protein after pouring it over. For one hour, cover and chill.

In a large skillet, heat the oil over medium-high heat. Place the pork in the heated pan after removing it from the marinade and storing it.

Cook until the outside is beautifully browned. Add the dried onion, orange juice, 1/2 cup water, and the set-aside marinade. Simmer for about 30 minutes, or until the pork is tender to the fork, on low heat with the lid on.

Mix the flour and two tablespoons of water in a small cup. Stir into the skillet, then cook it uncovered for 2 to 4 minutes until it has thickened.

PAPAS A LA HUANCAINA (POTATOES IN A SPICY CHEESE SAUCE)

Prep Time:15 mins
Cook Time: 20 mins
Total Time: 35 mins
Servings: 4 to 6 s

Ingredients

- Eight medium yellow or white potatoes peeled
- Eight large black olives, halved
- Lettuce leaves
- Huancaína sauce
- Two large hard-boiled eggs

Directions

Connect the components. The potatoes are added after boiling a big pot of salted water. Boil the potatoes for 15 to 20 mins or up to they can be easily pierced with a fork. Potatoes must be dried out and allowed to cool. Place the sliced potatoes on the lettuce leaves.

Add black olive halves and slices of hard-boiled egg as garnish on top of the potatoes after adding Huancaina sauce.

BESOS DE MOZA: PERUVIAN CANDIES

Prep Time: 15 mins
Cook Time: 45mis
Total Time: 60mins
Servings: 24

Ingredients

- 12 oz semisweet chocolate, chopped
- 24-round vanilla cookies
- ½ tablespoons unflavored gelatin
- Six egg whites at room temperature
- 1 ½ cup sugar

Directions

Chocolate should be melted in a water bath. Add gelatin to 1/4 cup of cold water. Place it over low heat to fully dissolve once it has partially dissolved. Place aside.

Egg whites should be combined with sugar in the bowl of an electric mixer, placed over a water bath, and whisked with a wire whisk or spatula until the sugar is dissolved and the egg whites are warm. We don't want to cook the egg whites, so don't overheat them. Avoid doing this near an intense heat source.
The electric mixer beats at high speed until the meringue is glossy and smooth. While the mixture is still warm, add the melted gelatin and beat until all the ingredients are mixed, and the meringue has cooled and become firm.

Brush them with oil if you can locate molds to produce besos de moza. Pour the hot chocolate and scoop off any extra to leave a thin coating. Fill the chocolate molds with meringue after adding it to a piping bag with a big nozzle. Lastly, have a vanilla cookie. After cooling for a few while, remove from molds.

Place cookies on a rack on a baking pan if you don't have any molds. Each cookie should have a dollop of meringue on top, about 1 1/2 inches high, added with the piping bag. Pour enough chocolate to coat the meringue thoroughly. The tray below will receive the spilled liquid. Refrigerate the chocolate until it becomes solid.

They're best when fresh, but you can store them in the fridge for a few days.

POLLO A LA PINA

Prep Time: 25 mins
Cook Time: 25 mins
Total Time: 50 mins

Ingredients

- 1 ½ tablespoons soy sauce
- One teaspoon salt
- Two tablespoons of tomato paste
- One red bell pepper, cored and sliced
- Three green onions sliced
- ½ teaspoon ground black pepper
- ½ teaspoon garlic powder
- ½ teaspoon ground cumin
- Three boneless, skinless chicken breasts cut into bite-sized medallions
- 20-ounce pineapple chunks in syrup
- 1 ½ cups white sugar
- 2 cups potato starch, or as needed
- One tablespoon of vegetable oil
- One teaspoon of vegetable oil

Directions

In a large bowl made of glass or ceramic, combine the soy sauce, cumin, salt, pepper, and garlic powder. Chicken medallions should be added and coated evenly. To marinate, set away. Combine the sugar, syrup, and pineapple chunks; boil. Boil for 2-3 mins or until sugar is dissolved.

Put pineapple chunks in a container, remove them from the heat, and keep the syrup in the saucepan. In a bowl, add potato starch. Chicken medallions that have been marinated are coated in potato starch; extra is shaken off.

Warm one tablespoon of vegetable oil in a large skillet set over medium-high heat. In batches, add the chicken and fry it for about 3 minutes per side until golden brown and crispy. If required, add additional oil. Move to a platter covered with paper towels.

In a wok, heat the final teaspoon of vegetable oil. Tomato paste should be added and cooked, and stirred until it darkens. Add bell pepper and heat for 1 to 2 minutes or until slightly softened but crunchy. Combine with pineapple chunks and chicken medallions. Until the mixture is faintly coated, slowly incorporate some of the syrup; save the remaining syrup for later use. Add some green onions on top.

Notes

If you like, corn starch can be substituted for potato starch.

CHICKEN, CHICKPEA, AND VEGETABLE STEW

Prep Time: 15 mins
Cook Time:1 hr 15 mins
Total Time: 1 hr 30 mins
Servings: 4

Ingredients

- 2 tbsp extra virgin olive oil
- Four chicken thighs, bone-in, skin on
- 1/4 tsp turmeric
- Pinch cayenne
- 1/3 cup chopped cilantro (or substitute flat leaf parsley), divided
- One onion peeled
- Two carrots peeled
- 3-4 garlic cloves, crushed
- 1 cup chicken broth
- 1 3/4 cups ripe diced tomatoes
- 1 3/4 cups cooked chickpeas
- One roasted red bell pepper, skinned and sliced
- 1 tsp smoked paprika
- 1/2 tsp cumin
- Salt and pepper

Direction

Lightly sprinkle chicken thighs with salt & pepper. Heat the olive oil in a sauté pan with high faces until hot. Keep the heat medium-high and add the chicken thighs, skin-side down, to the heated oil. The thighs must be cooked for approximately 10 minutes, turning them once halfway through or until the skin is golden and crisp and the thighs are browned on both sides. Take the thighs out of the pan. Don't remove the pan's juices or fat.

Include the minced onion in the pan, and cook for 5 to 8 minutes or until softened. Add the carrots and sauté them for 5 minutes when the onion caramelizes. As the mixture cooks, toss the garlic and cook for 2 minutes, stirring often to ensure the garlic becomes fragrant.

Add three tablespoons of chopped cilantro or parsley, chicken broth, diced tomatoes, chickpeas, roasted bell pepper, smoked paprika, cumin, turmeric, and cayenne. Cayenne must only be used sparingly when added to taste because it is hot. Cayenne spice, which I love to add, gives the stew a good spicy kick and 1/4 teaspoon.

The mixture must be stirred before boiling. As desired, season with salt and pepper (I often put around 12 tsp of salt, but it depends on how salty my chicken broth is). Simmer the heat down. Put the chicken thighs in the sauté pan and cover them with sauce. Stirring occasionally, cover the pot with the vent on one side, and boil the stew for 45 minutes.

Open the pot's lid. Until the liquid is reduced and the sauce begins to thicken, simmer for a further 15 minutes. Take the sauce-coated chicken thighs out of the oven. Remove and discard the skin. Slice the flesh thinly off the bones. Discard any extra fat and bones.

Stirring together, add the chicken shreds back to the sauté pan. Simmer until the sauce is thoroughly heated or has reached the desired consistency. Add a little chicken stock to moisten the stew if it appears to be too dry.
Remove from the pan and top with the final two tablespoons of chopped cilantro. Serve the cooked quinoa, couscous, or brown rice with the chicken-chickpea stew.

PERUVIAN BELUGA LENTILS WITH BEET PUREE

Prep Time: 15 minutes
Cook Time: 45 minutes
Total Time: 1 hour
Servings: 4

Ingredients

For the Peruvian lentil spice blend:
- 1/8 tsp ground cinnamon
- 1/8 tsp ground nutmeg
- ¼ tsp dried oregano
- ½ tsp ground cumin
- ¼ tsp ground black pepper
- 1/8 tsp ground white pepper
- For the Peruvian beluga lentils:
- 1 tbsp olive oil
- 2 cups white or yellow onion diced
- Three and ½ cups of low-sodium vegetable broth
- ½ cup plain, unsweetened non-dairy milk
- 3 tbsp aji amarillo paste
- Three cloves garlic minced
- One and ½ cups dried beluga lentils

For the beetroot puree:
- 8 oz Yukon gold potatoes slice into 2-inch pieces
- 24 oz red beets slice into 2-inch pieces
- ¾ tsp salt
- 2 tbsp freshly-squeezed lime juice
- 2 tbsp olive oil
- cooked brown rice
- vegetables of choice
- chopped fresh scallions

Directions

Heat the olive oil in a sizable saucepan (cast iron is preferred if you have it) over medium-high heat for the Peruvian beluga lentils. When the onion is softened and slightly browned, add the diced onion and cook, turning regularly, for 5 to 7 minutes. If necessary, include a little extra olive oil.

After adding the garlic, cook for another 60 seconds. Stir in all the spices, if using, and simmer for 30 seconds or until fragrant. Lentils and vegetable broth must be added. Once the mixture has come to a boil, cover the pan and simmer for a while.

Stirring periodically; cook for 25 minutes before adding the soy milk. For a further 10 to 20 minutes, simmer the lentils slightly covered. When the mixture starts to dry up, stir it occasionally and add vegetable broth, 1/4 cup at a time.
Add the paste made from aji amarillo. Add extra chili paste and salt and pepper to taste.

Steam the beets and potatoes to prepare the puree. Add water, the steaming rack, the beets, and the potatoes to a pressure cooker, such as an Instant Pot, and cook at high pressure for 15 minutes. If not, prepare your steamer and cook the food for 35 to 50 minutes or until it's fork-tender.

Peels should quickly come off once they are cold enough to handle. Add the salt and lime juice to a blender or food processor. Blend while gradually including the olive oil until uniform. Set aside after seasoning with a taste.

Prepare a bowl and any additional serving utensils. A quarter of the lentils, a quarter of the puree, and any garnishes should be added. Enjoy it hot. After they have cooled, leftovers can be kept in the fridge for about a week.

ORANGE AND PAPAYA JUICE

Prep Time: 10 mins
Servings: 4

Ingredients

- 2 cups fresh orange juice
- crushed ice Method
- 2 cups roughly chopped papaya
- 1/2 cup thick coconut milk

Directions

To make it:
1. Put all the ingredients in a mixer and process until smooth, leaving out the ice.
2. Include a few pieces of ice in each glass.
3. Over it, pour the papaya orange beverage.

The papaya orange cocktail should be served right away.

VEGAN CEVICHE

Prep Time: 15 mins
Total Time: 15 mins
Servings: 8

Ingredients

- 398ml hearts of palm drained and chopped into ½-inch pieces
- One sheet nori finely chopped
- tortilla chips 3 - 4 limes juiced
- One avocado cut into small cubes
- 1 cup cherry tomatoes quartered
- ¼ red onion finely sliced
- ½ cup cilantro roughly chopped

- ½ - 1 jalapeño finely chopped
- ½ teaspoon salt
- 1/4 teaspoon black pepper

Directions

Hearts of palm, nori, three limes' amount of juice, avocado, cherry tomatoes, red onion, cilantro, jalapenos, salt, and pepper to taste must all be added to a big bowl and gently combined. If desired, add extra lime juice after tasting. Along with tortilla chips, serve fresh.

Notes

Nori: The seaweed used to make sushi, nori gives sushi its fishy flavor. You can eliminate it for a less intense taste if you'd like. Use kitchen scissors to quickly and easily cut the nori into tiny flakes.

PUMPKIN STEW WITH VEGETABLES AND FAVA BEANS

Prep Time:10 mins
Cook Time:45 mins
Total Time:55 mins
Servings: 4

Ingredients
- 1 cup quinoa cooked
- Four aji verde peppers seeds removed, chopped
- 2 cups fresh or frozen fava beans
- One red onion chopped
- Seven cloves garlic chopped
- Four tablespoons extra virgin olive oil
- 2 cups chopped collard greens
- 3 cups diced pumpkin, butternut squash
- 2 cups diced peeled potatoes
- One tablespoon of curry powder
- One tablespoon cumin
- salt to taste

- Two ears of corn, each cut into four segments

Directions

Quinoa must be prepared as directed on the box. Aji peppers, garlic, onions, and olive oil are combined in a blender. Until smooth, puree. Add the pepper mixture to the heated big saucepan over medium-high heat. After 5 to 6 minutes of cooking, they were sometimes stirred.

Put potatoes in a different pot and add water to cover them. Bring to a boil and cook up to soft but not falling apart when examined with a fork. Save the water after draining the potatoes.

Add pumpkin dice. Cook the pumpkin for 10-15 minutes or until it has softened. Mash the pumpkin into a puree with a spatula. Add 2 cups of the potato water you set aside. Put corn in. Curry, cumin, and salt are optional. Boil, then turn down the heat and simmer.

Fava beans should be added to a different pot, covered with water, and cooked until soft. Reserve the fava bean water after draining. Fill the saucepan with 1 cup of fava bean water. Boil, then turn down the heat and simmer. Add potatoes, fava beans, and collard greens to the cooking vessel. Cook for a bit of time.

ANOVA CULINARY

Prep Time: 00:30 mins
Recipe Time: 6 mins

Ingredients

- 4-pound whole chicken, trussed
- 4 cups chicken stock
- One teaspoon of kosher salt
- One teaspoon of whole black peppercorns
- One dried bay leaf
- 2 cups diced carrots
- 2 cups diced celery
- 2 cups diced leek

Directions

Anova Sous Vide Precision Cooker should be set at 150°F (65°C). All components should be combined in a reasonably big zipper-lock bag. Place the bag in the water bath after using the water immersion technique to seal it. A six-hour timer was set. To reduce water evaporation, cover the water bath with plastic. Continually add water to keep the chicken submerged.

Keep the bag away from the water bath once the timer rings. Carefully remove the chicken from the bag. The cooking liquid has to be kept so that it may later be utilized in recipes as broth. It would be best if you turned the broiler too high. After patting the chicken dry, put it on a baking pan covered with foil. Broil the skin for 5 to 7 minutes or until golden brown. Slice and serve after 10 minutes of resting.

CILANTRO AND TURKEY SOUP

Prep Time: 10 mins
Cook Time: 40 mins
Total Time: 50 mins
Servings: 6

Ingredients

- Cilantro Paste
- 2 Tb aji amarillo
- One large bunch of cilantro
- ¼ cup water for thinning consistency
- One small bunch of fresh parsley
- Two garlic cloves roughly chopped
- ½ white onion roughly chopped
- Soup
- Two red-yellow bell peppers, chopped
- Two carrots peeled and chopped
- 1 cup frozen corn
- Salt and pepper
- Olive oil for drizzling
- Lime wedges for garnish
- ½ cup white rice uncooked
- ½ tsp cumin
- 2 Yukon gold potatoes chopped into 1-inch pieces
- 6 cups chicken or turkey stock
- 1 cup cooked turkey meat cubed or shredded
- 1 cup frozen peas

Directions

Make the paste first. The paste's components should be placed in a food processor or blender. Blend until thoroughly green and smooth. Place aside. In a large saucepan, sauté chopped carrots and bell pepper in olive oil until they soften, about 4 minutes.

Toss in the oil and uncooked rice. After that, mix the cumin with the cilantro paste to coat the rice. Potatoes, turkey, and turkey stock are then added. Salt and pepper are then added. Cook for about 30 minutes, or until the rice and potatoes are cooked, at a medium simmer. Add the frozen corn and peas, which cook quickly after the potatoes are soft. Add lime wedges as a garnish after ladling into dishes.

Notes

You can easily make this soup with leftover turkey or chicken.
Many Latin or Mexican markets have aji amarillo paste.

CONCLUSION

Peruvian cuisine is a vibrant and diverse blend of indigenous ingredients, Spanish influence, and African, Chinese, and Japanese immigrant cultures. The result is a delicious, spicy, and colorful culinary experience that has captivated food lovers worldwide.

We explored Peruvian cuisine's most popular and beloved dishes in this cookbook. We have covered traditional appetizers, main courses, and desserts, introducing you to the exotic ingredients and unique cooking techniques that make Peruvian food special.

One of the highlights of Peruvian cuisine is the use of indigenous ingredients cultivated in the Andes for centuries. These ingredients, such as quinoa, potatoes, corn, and ají peppers, are delicious and highly nutritious. They form the backbone of many Peruvian dishes, adding depth and complexity to the flavors.

In addition to the indigenous ingredients, Peruvian cuisine also features a range of seafood dishes that reflect the country's long coastline. The ceviche, for example, is a signature Peruvian dish that has become popular worldwide. This refreshing and zesty dish consists of raw fish marinated in lime juice and flavored with onions, cilantro, and ají peppers.

Another hallmark of Peruvian cuisine is using spices and herbs to create bold and complex flavors. The most popular spice in Peruvian cooking is aji amarillo, a bright yellow pepper with a fruity flavor and medium spiciness. It is used in many dishes, from soups to stews to marinades, and adds a distinctive flavor and color.

The cooking techniques used in Peruvian cuisine are also unique and varied. One of the most popular techniques is using the grill, or parrilla, to cook meat, chicken, and fish. This technique results in smoky and flavorful dishes, a Peruvian cuisine staple. Another popular style is using the clay pot, or cazuela, to cook stews and soups. This method ensures the food is cooked slowly and evenly, producing soft and flavorful dishes.

Finally, we must remember Peruvian desserts, which are just as delicious and diverse as the main courses. From the creamy and decadent tres leches cake to the refreshing and fruity mazamorra morada, Peruvian desserts are a perfect way to end any meal.

In conclusion, Peruvian cuisine is a unique and flavorful blend of indigenous ingredients, Spanish influence, and immigrant cultures. The food is spicy, colorful, and rich in flavor and reflects the country's diverse history and geography. We hope this cookbook has introduced you to some of the most beloved dishes in Peruvian cuisine and inspired you to try them at home. So go ahead and explore the flavors of Peru - you won't be disappointed!

PERUVIAN COOKING TIPS

Peruvian cuisine is known for its diverse flavors and cultural influences, ranging from indigenous Andean ingredients to Spanish, African, and Asian influences. Here are some Peruvian cooking tips to help you master the flavors of this delicious cuisine:

Experiment with Peruvian ingredients

Peruvian cuisine uses various unique ingredients not commonly used in other cuisines. These include ají amarillo (a spicy yellow pepper), huacatay (a black mint), choclo (Peruvian corn), quinoa (an Andean grain), and purple potatoes. Experimenting with these ingredients will help capture Peruvian cuisine's unique flavors and aromas.

Learn to make aji sauce

Aji sauce is a staple condiment in Peruvian cuisine and adds a spicy kick to dishes. To make aji sauce, blend ají amarillo peppers, garlic, lime juice, and salt until smooth. You can also add other ingredients like cilantro or onion for added flavor.

Use traditional cooking methods

Peruvian cuisine has a long history, and many traditional cooking methods are still used today. For example, the pachamanca is a conventional cooking method involving cooking meat, potatoes, and other ingredients in an underground pit with hot stones. Another traditional way is using a clay pot called a pachanga to cook stews and soups.

Make your own chicha morada

Chicha morada is a refreshing Peruvian drink from purple corn, pineapple, cinnamon, and cloves. To make your chicha morada, simmer purple corn, pineapple, cinnamon, and cloves in water for about an hour. Strain the liquid and add sugar and lime juice to taste.

Don't be afraid of spice

Peruvian cuisine is known for its bold and spicy flavors, and many dishes incorporate ají amarillo or other spicy ingredients. Don't be afraid to add heat to your dishes, but be mindful of your spice tolerance and your guests' preferences.

Use fresh ingredients

Fresh ingredients are vital to creating authentic Peruvian dishes. Use fresh herbs, spices, and vegetables to flavor your dishes whenever possible. If fresh ingredients are unavailable, look for high-quality frozen or dried options.

Incorporate seafood

Peru has a long coastline and is known for its seafood dishes. Incorporate seafood like shrimp, octopus, or fish into your Peruvian dishes to capture the flavors of the ocean.

Make ceviche

Ceviche is a traditional Peruvian dish from raw fish marinated in lime juice and spices. To make ceviche, marinate diced raw fish in lime juice, ají amarillo, garlic, salt, and pepper for 10-15 minutes. Add diced red onion, cilantro, and avocado for flavor and texture.

Try Peruvian-style fried rice

Peruvian-style fried rice, or arroz chaufa, is a popular dish in Peru that combines Chinese and Peruvian flavors. To make arroz chaufa, cook rice and set aside. Stir-fry diced vegetables, meats, and seafood with garlic and ginger in a separate pan. Add the cooked rice and stir-fry until everything is heated through.

Use Peruvian spices

Peruvian cuisine uses a variety of unique spices, including cumin, paprika, and oregano. Incorporate these spices into your dishes to add depth and complexity to the flavors.

THE END

Printed in France by Amazon
Brétigny-sur-Orge, FR